The Authors

Maralene and Miles Wesner are multi-talented teachers and prolific writers. They have published more than 150 Audio-Visual Education aids, and pioneered new reading methods with their Phonics in a Nutshell (1965).

They have written articles, and mission studies for Southern Baptist periodicals. They were in the original group of writers to develop WMU's Big "A" Club material.

They've published several books with Broadman Press: *A Fresh Look at the Gospel* (1983); *You Are What You Choose* (1984); and *How To Be a Saint When You Feel Like a Sinner* (1986) and self-published 30 books by Diversity Press.

They are noted for their no-nonsense style, their clear illustrations, and their willingness to face controversial issues. From the dual perspectives of both academic and religious professions, they seek to be a bridge between the spiritual and the intellectual worlds.

They hold Masters Degrees (MEd) from Oklahoma University plus work toward a Doctorate. Miles also attended Southwestern Baptist Theological Seminary, and served as a high school counselor. He has been the bi-vocational pastor of a small rural church for more than 50 years.

Both Maralene and Miles taught in public school and collages and served as educational consultants. Maralene taught Psychology and Speech for Southeastern Oklahoma State University for 32 years. She was chosen Oklahoma Teacher of the Year in 1975.

They have planned, led tours, and done research in all of the 50 states, Canada, Mexico, Europe, Egypt, Japan, and the Holy Land. In 1985, they were among a small group of Americans who were invited by Dr. Joseph P. Kennedy of the US/China Education Foundation and Bishop Ting, leader of the Three Self Movement, to participate in the First Symposium on the Church in Nanjing, China.

Now, they use their lifetime of varied experiences to write insightful sermons, essays, and books.

Titles by Maralene & Miles Wesner
published by Nurturing Faith

Sermons for Special Days

Life More Abundant

Do You Really Know Jesus?

If Jesus Were Here Today

101 Sparks of Inspiration

When God Can't Answer

Think (Or Else!)

Stumbling to Zion

Sensible Sermons

FINDING *Truth* IN THE PARABLES

Maralene & Miles Wesner

© 2023
Published in the United States by Nurturing Faith, Macon, GA.
Nurturing Faith is a book imprint of Good Faith Media (goodfaithmedia.org).
Library of Congress Cataloging-in-Publication Data is available.

ISBN: 978-1-63528-212-2

All rights reserved. Printed in the United States of America.

Scripture quotations are from New Revised Standard Version Bible Updated Edition, copyright © 2021 National Council of the Churches of Christ in the United States of America. Used by permission. All rights reserved worldwide.

Cover photograph by David Cassady.

Contents

Preface 1

1. Of Snakes and Temptations.. 3

2. Of Arks and Perseverance 9

3. Of Salt and Initiative.. 15

4. Of Sacrifices and Faith 21

5. Of Ladders and Grace 27

6. Of Coats and Forgiveness... 33

7. Of Burning Bushes and Commitment 39

8. Of Seas and Progress 45

9. Of Walls and Success.. 51

10. Of Giants and Service 57

11. Of Fiery Furnaces and Adversity 63

12. Of Lions and Courage.. 69

13 Of Handwriting and Warnings 75

14. Of Whales and Ministry 81

15. Of Angels and Salvation 87

Preface

The Bible is full of stories. Some are historical and factual, meant to be taken literally. Many others are parables about spiritual and moral issues, meant to teach a deeper lesson.

We don't necessarily know which stories are factual and which are not. Often, however, it doesn't matter; the meaning is what's important. Unless the story can be applied in our lives today, it's useless. Paul said, "All scripture is inspired by God and is useful for teaching, for reproof, for correction, and for training in righteousness" (2 Tim 3:16).

This verse tells us that the information in the Bible is there for a purpose. When we read or hear scripture, we must let it speak to us in a personal way. Unless the passage helps us answer our questions or solve our problems, then it's not God's word to us.

As we deal with fifteen of the most popular and well-known Bible stories, let's get beyond the facts to the meaning. The Bible is not a historical book or a scientific book; it's a theological book. The truth is in the lessons it teaches.

This way of studying the Bible requires both thought and prayer, but it's essential to Christian growth. Always ask the following questions: What is the purpose of this passage? Why was it included in the Bible? What deeper meaning is it trying to express? How can I apply this scripture in my everyday life? Most importantly, how can it speak to me today?

(If these parables are presented as a series of sermons or lessons, this Preface may need to be used as an introduction to explain the format and the purpose of each one.)

1.

Of Snakes and Temptations

One of the first stories in the Bible takes place in the garden of Eden:

> Now the serpent was more crafty than any other wild animal that the LORD God had made. He said to the woman, "Did God say, 'You shall not eat from any tree in the garden'?" The woman said to the serpent, "We may eat of the fruit of the trees in the garden, but God said, 'You shall not eat of the fruit of the tree that is in the middle of the garden, nor shall you touch it, or you shall die.'" But the serpent said to the woman, "You will not die, for God knows that when you eat of it your eyes will be opened, and you will be like God, knowing good and evil." So when the woman saw that the tree was good for food and that it was a delight to the eyes and that the tree was to be desired to make one wise, she took of its fruit and ate, and she also gave some to her husband, who was with her, and he ate. Then the eyes of both were opened, and they knew that they were naked, and they sewed fig leaves together and made loincloths for themselves. They heard the sound of the LORD God walking in the garden at the time of the evening breeze, and the man and his wife hid themselves from the presence of the LORD God among the trees of the garden. But the LORD God called to the man and said to him, "Where are you?" He said, "I heard the sound of you in the garden, and I was afraid, because I was naked, and I hid myself." He said, "Who told you that you were naked? Have you eaten from the tree of which I commanded you not to eat?" The man said, "The woman

whom you gave to be with me, she gave me fruit from the tree, and I ate." Then the LORD God said to the woman, "What is this that you have done?" The woman said, "The serpent tricked me, and I ate." (Gen 3:1–13)

Now, what is the purpose of this passage? What deeper meaning is it trying to express? Most importantly, how can it speak to us today?

Well, we are not going to meet any talking snakes! Furthermore, in the New Testament Jesus clearly explained that there are no literal forbidden fruits: "It is not what goes into the mouth that defiles a person, but it is what comes out of the mouth that defiles" (Matt 15:11). Therefore, it's obvious that the purpose of this story is to teach us an important lesson about temptation.

Temptation is something we face every day of our lives. In Bible times, the serpent stood for evil, and we are tempted by evil. Just as in Adam and Eve's case, our temptations are often attractive. They appear to have something good to offer. Otherwise, they wouldn't be temptations. For example, David was tempted by Bathsheba, who "was very beautiful" (2 Sam 11:2).

Things that are ugly and things that are obviously false and harmful aren't tempting. Few people eat mud. Few people steal garbage. Why? Because these things are not appealing. They aren't attractive. They aren't desirable. They don't fill needs.

Every unfilled need in a person's life is a potential temptation. If all needs were filled, there would be no temptation. If you're absolutely full, food isn't tempting.

Our temptations, like Eve's, will appear to be good. The scripture says, "When the woman saw that the tree was good for food and that it was a delight to the eyes and that tree was to be desired to make one wise, she took of its fruit and ate" (Gen 3:6).

Temptations are successful because they never look distasteful or dangerous on the surface. That's why we must always think about long-term effects and future consequences. We must avoid people, places, and situations that tempt us. Jesus said, "Stay awake and pray that you may not come into the time of trial" (Matt 26:41).

There is a legend that St. Augustine was accosted by a former mistress shortly after his conversion. He immediately turned and walked in the opposite direction. Surprised, the woman cried out, "Augustine, it is I." Augustine, proceeding on his way, called back to her, "Yes, I know. But it is not I." He meant that he was a new man, and this new Augustine would avoid the very appearance of evil. Notice that God's command was not merely that Adam and Eve should not eat of the fruit, but that they should not even touch it.

William Jennings Bryan told of a man who had been an alcoholic. He reformed and signed the pledge, but when he rode into town, he kept hitching his horse to the rail in front of the tavern. Soon, he was drunk again. The way to avoid evil is to avoid the very place and appearance of it.

Even so, avoidance won't always work. Every human being succumbs to temptation. John said, "If we say that we have no sin, we deceive ourselves" (1 John 1:8). Furthermore, what tempts one person may not tempt another. Fruit that is forbidden for one may not be forbidden for another. Some individuals may have to avoid alcohol; others may have to avoid fattening food. Some have problems with sexual perversion or material greed or pride. None of us can feel smug because we're not susceptible to our neighbor's sin. It's obvious that we have plenty of our own. They may be different, but they are just as wrong. James said, "Whoever keeps the whole law but fails in one point has become accountable for all of it" (Jas 2:10).

Examine yourself. What runs through your mind at your lowest points? What obsession dominates your thoughts? What negative belief takes over when you experience a disappointment? What is your bottom-line weakness that triggers all your other destructive behavior? Your "forbidden fruit" is whatever will harm you, influence you to make poor choices, diminish your joy and freedom, or break your spiritual connection.

So what should we do about our sin? Well, this story about Adam and Eve tells us what not to do. We must not deny and hide our sins. Hiding never helps. The problem remains and grows worse. Instead, when we do wrong, we must immediately admit it to ourselves, confess it to God, and accept responsibility for it. Solomon said, "No one who conceals transgressions will prosper, but one who confesses and forsakes them will obtain mercy" (Prov 28:13).

John said, "If we confess our sins, he who is faithful and just will forgive us our sins and cleanse us from all unrighteousness" (1 John 1:9).

We must not blame someone else or "pass the buck." Both Adam and Eve pointed fingers at others. Adam blamed God for giving him Eve, and he blamed Eve for making him eat. Then Eve blamed the snake.

We are created as autonomous individuals with free will. When we sin, we are the ones who are responsible, and we must accept that responsibility. James said, "One is tempted by one's own desire, being lured and enticed by it; then, when that desire has conceived, it engenders sin, and sin, when it is fully grown, gives birth to death" (Jas 1:14–15).

This story also teaches us that when we do wrong, we will suffer the consequences. As a result of their sin, Adam and Eve lost their position in the garden of Eden, and life became difficult. The same is true today. Sin always has consequences. Even forgiven sin has consequences. A drug addict can be forgiven, but his health will still suffer.

The last thing this story teaches us is that God forgives and redeems. When we succumb to temptation, all is not lost. Paul said, "God is faithful, and he will not let you be tested beyond your strength, but with the testing he will also provide the way out so that you may be able to endure it" (1 Cor 10:13).

God, through his grace, can enable us to use our mistakes and problems for good. They strengthen us and make us more mature. The scripture says, "Discipline always seems painful rather than pleasant at the time, but later it yields the peaceful fruit of righteousness to those who have been trained by it" (Heb 12:11).

Our flaws and faults can actually make us more understanding and helpful to others. Enduring temptation can make us more empathetic. The writer of Hebrews says, "Because he himself was tested by what he suffered, he is able to help those who are being tested" (Heb 2:18).

Now, what have we learned from this account of Adam and Eve in the garden of Eden? Unfortunately, the only thing most people know about this popular story is that there's a talking snake and an apple tree. If that's all we know, we've totally missed God's word to us.

Remember, Paul said, "Scripture is inspired by God and is useful for teaching" (2 Tim 3:16).

In order to make this scripture useful in our lives, we must discover and apply the deeper moral teachings. We must get beyond the literal words to the meaning.

First, we're advised to avoid and reject temptation. God said, "Don't eat it or even touch it." Jesus said, "Stay awake and pray that you may not come into the time of trial; the spirit indeed is willing, but the flesh is weak" (Matt 26:41).

Paul said, "Abstain from every form of evil" (1 Thess 5:22).

All of us have weaknesses and vulnerabilities. These will be our problem areas. We must learn to be careful and cautious in certain places, with certain people, and with certain types of situations.

Next, we're shown that when we do sin, hiding or blaming others is not helpful. Adam and Eve pointed fingers and then tried to hide. David responded differently: "I acknowledged my sin to you, and I did not hide my iniquity; I said, 'I will confess my transgressions to the LORD,' and you forgave the guilt of my sin" (Ps 32:5).

When we do make a mistake or render a poor decision, we must recognize it, analyze it, confess it to God, and deal with it as quickly as possible. We should accept responsibility and provide correction and restitution if that's appropriate.

Finally, we're warned about the terrible consequences of sin, but we're also given a promise that God's grace can enable us to overcome and even use our failures to grow and serve. James says, "My brothers and sisters, whenever you face various trials, consider it all joy, because you know that the testing of your faith produces endurance" (Jas 1:2–3).

Once we've done all we can to remediate our transgression, we must view it as a learning experience. It can help us overcome our own feelings of self-righteousness and teach us to be more understanding and tolerant of other sinners. After we've gone through these steps, then we should dismiss our mistakes and move on.

These are powerful lessons. Applying them in our lives every day makes this scripture real and allows God's word to speak to us.

2.

Of Arks and Perseverance

Every kindergarten child knows the story about Noah and the ark:

> Noah was a righteous man, blameless in his generation; Noah walked with God. And Noah had three sons: Shem, Ham, and Japheth. Now the earth was corrupt in God's sight, and the earth was filled with violence. And God saw that the earth was corrupt, for all flesh had corrupted its ways upon the earth. And God said to Noah, "I have determined to make an end of all flesh, for the earth is filled with violence because of them; now I am going to destroy them along with the earth. Make yourself an ark of cypress wood; make rooms in the ark, and cover it inside and out with pitch. This is how you are to make it: the length of the ark three hundred cubits, its width fifty cubits, and its height thirty cubits. Make a roof for the ark, and finish it to a cubit above, and put the door of the ark in its side; make it with lower, second, and third decks. For my part, I am going to bring a flood of waters on the earth, to destroy from under heaven all flesh in which is the breath of life; everything that is on the earth shall die. But I will establish my covenant with you, and you shall come into the ark, you, your sons, your wife, and your sons' wives with you. And of every living thing, of all flesh, you shall bring two of every kind into the ark, to keep them alive with you; they shall be male and female. Of the birds according to their kinds and of the animals according to their kinds, of every creeping thing of the ground according to its kind, two of every kind shall come in to you, to keep them alive."… Noah

did all that the LORD had commanded him.... Noah with his sons and his wife and his sons' wives went into the ark to escape the waters of the flood. (Gen 6:9–20; 7:5, 7)

Noah obeyed and saved his family and all living creatures. After forty days of rain and many days of waiting, the ordeal was over. As soon as the ark's passengers were on dry land again, Noah set up an altar of thanksgiving. God said, "As long as the earth endures, seedtime and harvest, cold and heat, summer and winter, day and night shall not cease" (Gen 8:22).

This was the assurance. As a sign of his promise never again to destroy the world with a flood, God set in the sky an arc of colors, the rainbow of mercy: "I have set my bow in the clouds, and it shall be a sign of the covenant between me and the earth" (Gen 9:13).

Now, what is the purpose of this passage? What deeper meaning is it trying to express? Most importantly, how can it speak to us today?

Well, no flood is going to destroy the whole world: "The waters shall never again become a flood to destroy all flesh" (Gen 9:15). It's also extremely unlikely that you will ever need to build an ark. It certainly wouldn't be possible for you to collect animals of every species. Therefore, in order for this account to have any practical application in our lives today, we must discover the deeper lesson it teaches.

This story is not really about animals and floods. It's about how a righteous man dealt with a life crisis through obedience and perseverance.

Noah was a man who listened to wise counsel. He planned and prepared for the future. He worked tirelessly and persistently, even in the face of opposition. Very few individuals do that in our modern world. We live in a "me now" culture. Research shows that only a small percentage of people think about tomorrow or feel the need to earn before they spend. Very few people practice "deferred gratification." Very few people get their priorities straight. Very few people emphasize what's really important. Very few people heed the scriptural warning that says, "Prepare to meet your God" (Amos 4:12).

Jesus believed in preparation. He said, "Which of you, intending to build a tower, does not first sit down and estimate the cost, to see whether he has enough to complete it?" (Luke 14:28).

Today, few people "count the cost." Loans and credit cards allow us to enjoy the "fruits" before the labor. That sets up a dangerous precedent. Most people wait until the rain comes before they think about fixing their leaking roof, but Noah didn't wait until the rains came before he began to build his ark. He was willing to prepare for a flood he couldn't see. The scripture says,

"By faith Noah, warned by God about events as yet unseen, respected the warning and built an ark to save his household; by this he condemned the world and became an heir to the righteousness that is in accordance with faith" (Heb 11:7).

Noah also practiced altruism and generosity. He thought beyond himself and his own selfish needs. He was willing to spend his life, his time, and his energy to provide security for his family and to salvage all living things. Few people care enough about our environment and natural resources to practice good stewardship. If something helps *me*, most of us aren't concerned about the rest of humanity. If something is pleasurable now, we don't care about those who will live in the decades to come. Paul said, "Let each of you look not to your own interests but to the interests of others" (Phil 2:4).

It's important to remember that Noah persevered. Paul could have used him as an example when he said, "Do not be weary in doing what is right" (2 Thess 3:13).

Noah kept working even in the face of ridicule and discouraging remarks. He was one man against the forces of public opinion. For many years he stood absolutely alone in an evil world.

Most of us are too easily swayed by those around us. We are persuaded by polls and media hype. But Noah believed in his project and was dedicated to his task. He didn't become discouraged when no one listened to him. Jesus said, "As in the days before the flood they were eating and drinking, marrying and giving in marriage, until the day Noah entered the ark" (Matt 24:38).

It's the same today. There is evil all around us. Problems abound. We have wars, murders, violence, and hatred. Yet for many people life goes on with very little thought for the future.

So how can we listen to God's voice as Noah did? How can we plan, prepare, and persevere as Noah did? How can we overcome adversity in a chaotic world? How can we handle life's crises? Will we let them destroy us, or will we, like Noah, have the determination and perseverance necessary to prevail? The ark enabled Noah and his family to rise above circumstances.

We must not drown in the floods of evil and destruction; we must overcome them. In order to do this, we need spiritual guidance. We need perseverance. Too many of us follow the path of least resistance. We're lazy and apathetic. We say, "I don't want to get involved"; "I can't be bothered"; "It's just too much trouble."

We are irresponsible and undependable. We forget. We let things go. We run out of time. We lose interest. We get tired. We give up. We chose pleasure today instead of preparation for tomorrow.

Idleness is life's worst enemy. Phillip Brooks said, "It doesn't take great men to do great things. It only takes ordinary men with great dedication." Noah had dedication and perseverance.

Most people avoid physical exertion. They prefer to wait for a windfall. But that rarely happens. A businessman said, "Every time I hear the word 'lucky' applied to one of my successful employees, I think of all the things he did that others wouldn't do and of all the years he had been doing them. When a truck needed to be driven, he drove it. When an order needed to be delivered, he delivered it. When the work went past midnight, he stayed until the job was done. He always managed to be in the right place at the right time. People who achieve greatness seem to have that kind of 'luck.'"

Paul may have been thinking of Noah when he said, "Let us not grow weary in doing what is right, for we will reap at harvest time, if we do not give up" (Gal 6:9).

Adversity and floods are inevitable, and all of us will eventually need a place of safety. But we must plan and prepare if we expect to be ready for unexpected crises. Have you built an ark? Do you have a place of safety? Are you preparing for the future?

How can we apply this story about Noah to our own lives today? Well, everyone depends upon something. The rich man may depend upon his wealth. The intellectual may depend upon his education. The soldier may depend upon his weapons. The athlete may depend upon his strength. What do you depend upon? What gives you a feeling of security when you're threatened? What do you rely on to calm your fears? What thoughts help you when you're under stress?

In hours of need, some people pray. Others read scriptures. Church members may talk to their pastor and Christian friends. Our ark is whatever we rely on when we're desperate.

Are you depending on a leaky boat that will let you down in rough water, or are you depending on a sure and eternal ark? Material things will let you down. People will let you down. Only God is sure and certain.

Now, what have we learned from this story of Noah and his ark? Unfortunately, when they hear the word *ark*, most people think of two elephants and two giraffes. If that's our only understanding, we've totally missed God's word to us.

Remember, Paul said, "Scripture is inspired by God and is useful for teaching" (2 Tim 3:16).

To make this scripture useful in our lives, we must discover and apply the deeper moral teachings. We must get beyond the literal words to the meaning.

First, we're told to plan, prepare, and persevere in order to ensure security in our future. Jesus said, "You will have affliction. Be faithful until death, and I will give you the crown of life" (Rev 2:10).

Noah didn't neglect the important things. He didn't procrastinate. His commitment and hard work paid off. He devoted his life to a task that proved to be worthwhile. His faith was vindicated. He was safe. He protected his family, and he blessed the world.

Like Noah, each of us has a mission that requires dedication and perseverance. Being faithful means staying focused, ignoring distractions, and accomplishing our task.

Next, we're encouraged to take responsibility for the safety of our family and our world. Paul said, "We who are strong ought to put up with the failings of the weak and not to please ourselves. Each of us must please our neighbor for the good purpose of building up the neighbor" (Rom 15:1–2).

Selfishness is an ever-present sin. Most of us are concerned with what's good for me now. But we are our brothers' and sisters' keeper as well as helper. We must think of others. We are also caretakers of our planet's resources. Good stewardship is a Christian obligation.

Finally, we're assured that God will reward our obedience and perseverance. The scripture says, "Noah found favor in the sight of the LORD" (Gen 6:8).

We can also find favor and grace. John said, "The law indeed was given through Moses; grace and truth came through Jesus Christ" (John 1:17).

The idea of grace includes all that is joyful, beautiful, and favorable. This is the first time this special attribute of God is emphasized in the scriptures. It is also our gift when we faithfully persevere.

These are powerful lessons. Applying them in our lives every day makes this scripture real and allows God's word to speak to us.

3.

Of Salt and Initiative

A rather strange Bible story tells about a couple who must leave their home to avoid a disaster. Lot made it to safety, but his wife looked back and became a pillar of salt. The scripture says,

> The angels urged Lot, saying, "Get up, take your wife and your two daughters who are here, or else you will be consumed in the punishment of the city." But he lingered, so the men seized him and his wife and his two daughters by the hand, the LORD being merciful to him, and they brought him out and left him outside the city. When they had brought them outside, they said, "Flee for your life; do not look back or stop anywhere in the plain; flee to the hills, or else you will be consumed." And Lot said to them, "Oh, no, my lords; your servant has found favor with you, and you have shown me great kindness in saving my life, but I cannot flee to the hills, for fear the disaster will overtake me and I die. Look, that city is near enough to flee to, and it is a little one. Let me escape there—is it not a little one?—and my life will be saved!" He said to him, "Very well, I grant you this favor too and will not overthrow the city of which you have spoken. Hurry, escape there, for I can do nothing until you arrive there." Therefore the city was called Zoar. The sun had risen on the earth when Lot came to Zoar. Then the LORD rained on Sodom and Gomorrah sulfur and fire from the LORD out of heaven, and he overthrew those cities and all the plain and all the inhabitants of the cities and what grew on the ground. But Lot's wife, behind him, looked back, and she became a pillar of

salt. Abraham went early in the morning to the place where he had stood before the LORD, and he looked down toward Sodom and Gomorrah and toward all the land of the plain and saw the smoke of the land going up like the smoke of a furnace. So it was that, when God destroyed the cities of the plain, God remembered Abraham and sent Lot out of the midst of the overthrow, when he overthrew the cities in which Lot had settled. (Gen 19:14–29)

Now, what is the purpose of this passage? What deeper meaning is it trying to express? Most importantly, how can it speak to us today?

Well, the city you live in probably won't ever be totally destroyed. Furthermore, people don't suddenly turn into pillars of salt. So of what value is this scripture to us now?

It's obvious that the purpose of this story is to teach us an important lesson about obedience and initiative. In fact, there are many ways of looking back. After a crisis or a tragedy or a major milestone in our lives, most of us do look back. We may say, "Why did I do that?" or "If only I had done this" or "I wish I'd made a different choice!"

We spend endless hours second-guessing our former decisions and actions. Such regrets, guilts, and fears can cause us to become just as paralyzed or petrified as a pillar of salt. These useless attitudes stifle our initiative. If we keep living in the past, we'll never grow or make progress. All of us experience catastrophes. All of us suffer losses and adversities. All of us come to moments of truth when we must make hard choices. All of us face situations that force us to accept responsibility for our own behavior. All of us have to make important decisions. At these times we can either stop and look back or we can keep looking forward and move on.

The writer of Hebrews gave an even sterner warning about hesitating or abandoning a positive life choice: "It is impossible to restore again to repentance those who have once been enlightened and have tasted the heavenly gift and have shared in the Holy Spirit and have tasted the goodness of the word of God and the powers of the age to come and then have fallen away, since on their own they are crucifying again the Son of God" (Heb 6:4–6).

Jesus said, "No one who puts a hand to the plow and looks back is fit for the kingdom of God" (Luke 9:62).

When the writer of Hebrews says *fallen away* and when Jesus mentions *looking back*, what did they mean? Well, they didn't mean considering or analyzing our past behavior. They didn't mean recalling our successes. They didn't mean remembering our joys. Those are legitimate ways of dealing with the past. Instead, they meant having second thoughts after we've taken a moral stand. They meant ceasing to grow when we encounter difficulties. They meant giving up and quitting after we've begun a worthwhile project. They meant failing to follow through on our spiritual commitments.

We may look back by trying to relive the past. We may look back by allowing shame for our failures to destroy our initiative. We may look back by searching for an easier path when the going gets tough.

But looking back inevitably stymies us and hardens us. When we let the past contaminate the present, we lose our possibility of victory. Regret and guilt cause inner conflict. Arguing about unfinished business ruins relationships. Rehashing negative events is useless. In the case of moral and spiritual failures, there is forgiveness. With the slate wiped clean, we can look to the future. We don't have to stop living when we recall our former faults and sins. Lot's wife had a chance for a new, safe, and happy life, but she disobeyed and looked back. A pillar of salt represents something that is fixated and set. A pillar of salt is not growing. A pillar of salt is not moving. A pillar of salt is not living.

That's the symbolic message in this account. If we keep looking back, we will never reach our potential.

Lot's wife was stuck on the plains; she never reached the mountain. Are there things in your past that draw you back? Do you have uncertainty and doubts? Does the temptation to give up take over? Have you failed to fulfill your commitments? Have you broken your promises? Have you "fallen away" from the joy of your salvation? If so, you've turned into a pillar of salt.

So what can we learn from Lot's wife? We can realize that our past often becomes an obstacle to our future. We can understand that grief, regret, and longing for the "good old days" keep us from moving on with our lives. Remember, Paul had murdered Christians and tried to destroy the church, but after his conversion he wrote, "One thing I have laid hold of: forgetting what lies behind…I press on toward the goal" (Phil 3:13–14).

Like Paul, we too can quit wallowing in guilt. Of course we have made decisions we wish we could change. We have said words we wish we could take back. We have done deeds we wish we could undo. But changing the past is impossible. Instead, we can believe the scripture that says, "If anyone is in Christ, there is a new creation: everything old has passed away; look, new things have come into being!" (2 Cor 5:17). Guilt is only useful if it makes us confess our sins, rectify our mistakes, and change our behavior.

The truth of the Christian gospel is that we can always start anew. When Thomas Edison's factory burned in 1914, the great inventor's dreams seemed to be going up in smoke. His son Charles said, "My heart ached for him. Here he was, sixty-seven years old, and everything he had worked for was in ashes."

Nevertheless, the next morning when Edison looked at the ruins, he said, "There's value in disaster. All our mistakes are burned up. Thank God we can start anew."

What a wonderful attitude. When a business fails or a job is lost or a personal ambition is dashed, there is always a chance to learn from our mistakes and start over. We need to say, "The past is gone. There is nothing I can do to change it." One writer gives this advice in an old poem:

> I've shut the door on yesterday—
> > Its sorrow and mistakes.
> > And now I throw the key away
> > As each new dawn awakes.
> I've shut the door on yesterday
> > And thrown the key away.
> > Tomorrow holds no fears for me
> > Since I have found today.

As Christians, we must leave the former things, show initiative, and go forward!

Once, a skiing family was on a mountain when a blizzard blew a cold wind into their faces. The six-year-old son said, "Daddy, I don't want to go in this direction. It's too hard."

Even so, they had to ski in that direction to get back to their car. Once they had made it, the little boy said, "Hey, we did it!" His sense of pride showed that sometimes the only way to accomplish something in life is to "head into the wind" and keep moving.

Jesus did that when he "set his face" toward Jerusalem and his crucifixion (see Luke 9:51).

Now, what have we learned from this story about Lot and his wife? Unfortunately, most people just think it's a strange account about a woman turning into a pillar of salt. If that's our only understanding, we've totally missed God's word to us.

Remember, Paul said, "Scripture is inspired by God and is useful for teaching" (2 Tim 3:16).

To make this scripture useful in our lives, we must discover and apply the deeper moral teachings. We must get beyond the literal words to the meaning.

First, we've learned that there will be times in our lives when we must leave the past behind and move on with an attitude of hope and expectation. Paul said, "Set your minds on the things that are above, not on the things that are on earth" (Col 3:2). Living in the past is not productive. We can't drive safely by constantly looking in the rearview mirror. Almost every scriptural hero had a negative and sinful past. David committed adultery and murder. Paul persecuted the church. Peter lied and denied Jesus. But they went on to accomplish great things, and so can we.

Next, instead of asking, "Why did this happen?" we can show initiative by asking, "What do I need to do now?" The scripture says, "Whatever your hand finds to do, do with your might" (Eccl 9:10). Looking forward and staying busy is much better than wallowing in guilt and regret. Remorse and depression stymie initiative. Action and optimism encourage initiative.

Finally, we are assured that if we're obedient, God's grace will protect and support us just as it did Lot. Paul said, "The Lord is faithful; he will strengthen you and guard you from the evil one" (2 Thess 3:3).

God never promises to protect disobedience. If you break the law of gravity, you will fall. If you stand out in a thunderstorm, you may be struck by lightning. God only protects us when we heed his advice, follow his laws, and obey his commands. Lot's wife was at the wrong place at the wrong time. She made a bad decision; that's why she was not protected. Lot went to the designated safe place; that's why he was protected.

These are powerful lessons. Applying them in our lives every day makes this scripture real and allows God's word to speak to us.

4.

Of Sacrifices and Faith

One of the most confusing stories in the Bible concerns Abraham and Isaac:

> [God] said, "Take your son, your only son Isaac, whom you love, and go to the land of Moriah and offer him there as a burnt offering on one of the mountains that I shall show you." So Abraham rose early in the morning, saddled his donkey, and took two of his young men with him and his son Isaac; he cut the wood for the burnt offering and set out and went to the place in the distance that God had shown him. On the third day Abraham looked up and saw the place far away. Then Abraham said to his young men, "Stay here with the donkey; the boy and I will go over there; we will worship, and then we will come back to you." Abraham took the wood of the burnt offering and laid it on his son Isaac, and he himself carried the fire and the knife. And the two of them walked on together. Isaac said to his father Abraham, "Father!" And he said, "Here I am, my son." He said, "The fire and the wood are here, but where is the lamb for a burnt offering?" Abraham said, "God himself will provide the lamb for a burnt offering, my son." And the two of them walked on together. When they came to the place that God had shown him, Abraham built an altar there and laid the wood in order. He bound his son Isaac and laid him on the altar on top of the wood. Then Abraham reached out his hand and took the knife to kill his son. But the angel of the LORD called to him from heaven and said, "Abraham, Abraham!" And he said, "Here I am." He said, "Do not lay your hand

on the boy or do anything to him, for now I know that you fear God, since you have not withheld your son, your only son, from me." And Abraham looked up and saw a ram, caught in a thicket by its horns. Abraham went and took the ram and offered it up as a burnt offering instead of his son. (Gen 22:2–13)

Now, what is the purpose of this passage? What deeper meaning is it trying to express? Most importantly, how can it speak to us today?

Well, be assured you won't ever be told to kill your child. Human sacrifice is not practiced today as it was in Old Testament times. This is such a startling account because it contradicts everything we know of God. All principles of morality tell us we're not to kill. The Ten Commandments definitely forbid it, saying, "You shall not murder" (Exod 20:13). Jesus even said, "If any of you cause one of these little ones who believe in me to sin, it would be better for you if a great millstone were fastened around your neck and you were drowned in the depth of the sea" (Matt 18:6).

Therefore, it's obvious that the purpose of this story is to teach us an important lesson about faith. These early writers seem to indicate that God was testing Abraham's faith, yet James says, "No one, when tempted, should say, 'I am being tempted by God,' for God cannot be tempted by evil and he himself tempts no one" (Jas 1:13).

Jesus came to reveal the truth about God. He said, "Whoever has seen me has seen the Father" (John 14:9).

The true God, revealed by Jesus, doesn't trick us or play games with us. The true God is omniscient. He didn't need to "test" Abraham's faith in order to know his heart. Therefore, in order to benefit from this story, we must understand the background to this passage.

Abraham was known for his faith. The scriptures say, "By faith Abraham obeyed when he was called to set out for a place that he was to receive as an inheritance, and he set out, not knowing where he was going" (Heb 11:8).

It was by faith that Abraham became a father. That's why, when God suddenly seems to say, "Abraham, take Isaac, your beloved son, and offer him as a burnt offering," this sets up a contradictory situation. Isaac had been promised. His children and grandchildren had been promised. How could these things come to pass if he were dead? Nevertheless, Abraham held on to his faith.

In order to understand, we must analyze the culture of the time. Human sacrifice had been practiced in the area of Abraham's birth. Also, neighboring tribes that did practice human sacrifice probably taunted Abraham about his lack of dedication to his God by withholding his child. These conditions led to his perception of God's command.

At the last minute, however, God speaks clearly, saying, "Do not lay your hand on the boy or do anything to him, for now I know that you fear God, since you have not withheld your son, your only son, from me" (Gen 22:12). Later, Jesus makes a similar statement, saying, "Whoever loves son or daughter more than me is not worthy of me" (Matt 10:37).

These verses seem to be describing a selfish, jealous God. But Jesus is really explaining that God must take first place. Then all the other "loves" will not be diminished. Instead, they will be enriched. If some other object or person takes first place, then it's not really love. It's greed or envy or pride.

God does expect and reward faith. Faith is believing in more than you can see, and Abraham did this. In fact, he indicated hope for God's intervention when he spoke to his servants, saying, "The boy and I will go over there; we will worship, and then we will come back to you" (Gen 22:5).

Also, when Isaac asked about a sacrifice, Abraham answered, "God himself will provide the lamb for a burnt offering" (Gen 22:8).

The writer of Hebrews goes further and says, "He considered the fact that God is able even to raise someone from the dead" (Heb 11:19).

James sums it up by saying, "Abraham believed God, and it was reckoned to him as righteousness" (Jas 2:23).

So how can we apply this story to our lives today? Well, as human beings we are never sure of our dedication until it's tested by adversity. Hard choices help us confirm our sense of priorities. Sometimes we have to be "pushed" before we discover we can fly. There's an old legend about an eagle that depicts this: "Come to the cliff," the mother bird said. But the eaglets hesitated, saying, "We're afraid." The mother repeated her command. They came. She pushed them. And they flew.

Likewise, let's make one thing clear: Testing times do not benefit God, who knows all things. Instead, they benefit us. Most of us fail to take our spirituality seriously. A missionary once preached to people who had never heard the gospel. Afterward, the spokesman for the group politely explained, "We are most grateful to you for coming to our village. We have always believed in our own gods of clay, wood, and stone, but since we have heard your message, we most certainly want to believe in this Christian God also."

Now, before we criticize this man and say, "You can't believe in our Christian God and still keep all your other gods," we should examine our own attitudes and actions. In America, after hearing an evangelistic message, our thoughts could often be expressed this way: "We are most grateful to you for speaking in our church. We have always believed in our own gods of wealth, fame, and pleasure, but since we have heard your message, we most certainly want to believe in this Christian God also!" In short, most of us really want an "add-on religion" that doesn't actually require giving up anything.

Too frequently, we put God last, just as a certain pagan tribe did. When these people cut down a tall tree, they would use the best parts for their houses, tools, and canoes. From the inferior scraps that weren't really good for anything else, they carved their gods. Do we do that?

Well, everyone tends to idolize something. All of us wrap out lives around some core. It may be money, a career, a person, or even a hobby.

What have you sacrificed? How deep is your faith? Think about your concerns and interests and values. What comes first in your life? Have you considered priorities? Have you faced difficult decisions? Have you met adversity with determination? Have you looked forward with faith?

We want God to guarantee outcomes and show us the results before we trust him. But when you don't see a way, when you don't have any proof, and when you don't even have a hopeful sign but you believe anyway, that's faith. This story seems to say, "If we follow the light that we have in an honest effort to please God, then more light will come." We know that Abraham was not supposed to kill his child. Nevertheless, since he was faithful to follow the guidance that he sensed one step at a time, further enlightenment did come at the crucial moment when it was needed.

It's interesting to discover that the next revelation doesn't come until we've responded to the last revelation. We grow as we reach out and fulfill commitments.

Now, what have we learned from this account of Abraham and Isaac? Unfortunately, the only thing most people know about this well-known story is that Abraham planned to sacrifice Isaac on an altar. If that's all we know, we have totally missed God's word to us.

Remember, Paul said, "Scripture is inspired by God and is useful for teaching" (2 Tim 3:16).

To make this scripture useful in our lives, we must discover and apply the deeper moral teachings. We must get beyond the literal words to the meaning.

First, we have discovered that Abraham was sensitive to God's voice. He listened and tried to respond to spiritual guidance. The scripture says, "Listen, and hear my voice; pay attention, and hear my speech" (Isa 28:23).

Most of us become so concerned with everyday problems and so distracted by trivial affairs that we neglect spiritual matters and ignore deeper truth. We must be aware of more important things and remain open to divine guidance.

Next, we have discovered that Abraham faithfully followed God's lead as he perceived it, even when things appeared to be confusing and impossible. The scripture says, "To obey is better than sacrifice" (1 Sam 15:22).

Sometimes finding the right answers and solutions is a difficult task. It's not always easy to know God's will in every situation. Audible voices and visible instructions are seldom provided. We must use our conscience, our experience, and the information that's available to us and then take one step at a time.

Finally, we've learned that what we perceive to be God's word to us now may not be the final truth. Abraham kept believing that further enlightenment would come when he needed it and that all things would work together for good if he was faithful. Jesus said, "Nothing is hidden that will not be disclosed, nor is anything secret that will not become known and come to light. So pay attention to how you listen, for to those who have, more will be given" (Luke 8:17–18).

If we are honest and sincere about doing the right thing, we can trust that more wisdom will be provided as we proceed in faith.

These are powerful lessons. Applying them in our lives every day makes this scripture real and allows God's word to speak to us.

5.

Of Ladders and Grace

From their birth, Jacob and Esau were rivals. Though they were twins, they seemed to be exact opposites. Esau, the hunter, was his father Isaac's favorite. Jacob, the thinker, was his mother Rebekah's favorite. Because Esau was the first born, by law and custom he was entitled to the "birthright." Even so, both Jacob and his mother believed Jacob deserved that blessing.

After deceiving his father and cheating his brother, Jacob gained the inheritance but had to flee. In a state of guilt, fear, and loneliness, Jacob faced his future. The scripture says,

> [Jacob] came to a certain place and stayed there for the night, because the sun had set. Taking one of the stones of the place, he put it under his head and lay down in that place. And he dreamed that there was a stairway set up on the earth, the top of it reaching to heaven, and the angels of God were ascending and descending on it. And the LORD stood beside him and said, "I am the LORD, the God of Abraham your father and the God of Isaac; the land on which you lie I will give to you and to your offspring, and your offspring shall be like the dust of the earth, and you shall spread abroad to the west and to the east and to the north and to the south, and all the families of the earth shall be blessed in you and in your offspring. Know that I am with you and will keep you wherever you go and will bring you back to this land, for I will not leave you until I have done what I have promised you." (Gen 28:10–15)

Jacob was shocked. God must have known about his lies and betrayals. If so, then why did he offer such generous promises? Jacob's dream gave him his first glimpse of grace. That dream changed Jacob's life. He woke up a different person. The scripture says, "Jacob woke from his sleep and said, 'Surely the LORD is in this place—and I did not know it!'" (Gen 28:16).

Now, what is the purpose of this passage? What deeper meaning is it trying to express? Most importantly, how can it speak to us today?

Well, everybody dreams, but these dreams don't usually cause drastic changes in our character and lifestyle. The lesson in this story teaches us the power of grace.

Jacob's dream was significant. It was a lucid dream, a symbolic dream, an inspirational dream. The ladder seemed to reveal a connection between earth and heaven. Jacob felt he had met God and received grace, forgiveness, assurance, and the promise of a blessed future.

For Jacob this was a turning point. This dream prepared Jacob for his later conversion, which is expressed as a wrestling match (see Gen 32:24–30). Before this event, he had been deceitful and scheming and utterly selfish. Afterward, he felt unworthy and ashamed of what he had done. He made a personal dedication and received a transformation. Before, he had manipulated his mother, taken advantage of his brother, and lied to his father. Finally, he said, "God, my life is in your hands."

Before, he had experienced guilt, anxiety, uncertainty, and hostility. Finally, he had peace and serenity. He gave up self-will and accepted God's will. Later, God even gave him another name, and he lived up to it: "God said to him, 'Your name is Jacob; no longer shall you be called Jacob, but Israel shall be your name.' So he was called Israel" (Gen 35:10). Jacob, the old name, means "one who replaces by trickery." Israel, the new name, means "one who is a prince of God or one who rules for God." So Jacob had a new name, and he became a new person.

How did Jacob change? How did the insights he had received enable and inspire him to embrace spirituality? This is a matter of universal significance.

How does such a radical conversion take place? An Alcoholics Anonymous member explained it this way: "There are two principles involved. First, 'Act as if'; next, 'Practice makes perfect.'" God enables us, but we must be committed.

An ancient legend illustrates this process:

> Once upon a time a princess was searching for a husband. She wished to marry a man with a beautiful face who radiated kindness, honesty, and love.

Hearing of the royal quest, a criminal with an ugly face that reflected the opposite characteristics of cruelty, dishonesty, and hatred concocted a scheme to deceive the princess. He commissioned an artist to make him a wonderful mask. He wore it and appeared before the princess. Putting on an amazing performance, he managed to fool her completely. She decided to marry him. The engagement was announced, and the wedding was set for one year later. During all those months the criminal had to wear his mask and "play the part" of a perfect gentleman.

At first he was very uncomfortable trying to express these good qualities. It felt strange to be patient and gentle. Little by little, he began to behave in this manner out of habit.

As the wedding date drew near, the criminal realized his deceit would soon be discovered. By now, however, he was in love with the princess, so he decided to tell her the truth. Upon learning of the hypocrisy, at first she felt angry and betrayed. However, before banishing him from the kingdom forever, she said, "Remove your mask so I can see your real face."

He knelt humbly before her and removed the beautiful mask. The princess was astonished. "Why did you go to all that trouble to have a mask made exactly like your own face?" she asked. You see, the criminal had now become the kindly man he had tried to be for so long.

Our character defects can be slowly removed. If we are dishonest but begin to always tell the truth, we will become an honest person. If we are fearful but begin putting our trust in God, our fear will be removed. If we are hostile but begin to deliberately offer forgiveness, we will develop compassion. The more we "act as if," the more we will change from within to become the type of person we aspire to be.

William James said, "You don't sing because you are happy; you are happy because you sing." This is not hypocrisy. It's like a mother who is awakened in the middle of the night by her crying baby. Does she say, "Honey, I'm sorry I can't get up and tend to you right now because I just don't feel like changing your diaper, and I don't want to be a hypocrite"? No! Whether she feels like it or not, a loving mother gets up and changes and feeds the child, who now smiles, coos, and drops off to sleep.

Now, that mom probably feels great as she crawls back into bed. You always feel better—on the inside—when you have acted responsibly on the outside. Most of the good in this world is done by people who don't necessarily "feel like it."

Do your dreams have ladders? What insights have changed your life? How can we apply this story to our lives today? Have you ever manipulated or deceived anyone? Have you ever tried to take advantage of a situation? Have you ever bent the truth a little bit for a good cause? Have you ever had to leave a scene because of conflict or misunderstanding? Have you ever felt guilty or lonely or alienated? If so, you can identify with Jacob.

Have you ever had an experience of grace in which you felt you received more than you deserved? Have you ever had a moment of hope about the future that erased your regret about the past? Have you ever had an insight or a feeling that made you want to say, "Surely God is in this place, and I knew it not." If so, you can also identify with Jacob.

A dream or vision of ladders indicates our deep desire for a higher realm. It reveals our aspirations and hopes for eternal life. It means we wish to connect with God and experience spirituality.

What happened to Jacob can happen to us. If we see ourselves for what we are, then we can change. If we realize the unworthiness of our selfish scheming, then we can change. If we are truly sorry for the pain we have caused others, then we can change. If we admit we are capable of doing sinful things to get what we want, then we can change. If we heed the voice within that says, "I will bless you and be with you," then we can change. If we honestly say, "Lord, I'm ready for you to remove my defects," then we can change. That's what happened to Jacob.

Now, what have we learned from this account of Jacob and his dramatic dream? Unfortunately, the only thing most people know about this story is that a man saw angels on a ladder. If that's all we know, we've totally missed God's word to us.

Remember, Paul said, "Scripture is inspired by God and is useful for teaching" (2 Tim 3:16).

To make this scripture useful in our lives, we must discover and apply the deeper moral teachings. We must get beyond the literal words to the meaning.

First, we've learned that all human beings have faults and flaws. Paul said, "All have sinned and fall short of the glory of God" (Rom 3:23). No man or woman is perfect. No one always makes the best choices. No one achieves every goal they've set. That's okay! We have weaknesses and strengths. We have good traits and bad traits. Our knowledge is incomplete. We must accept ourselves as we are. That's what God does!

Next, we've learned that God's grace can change us and "rename us." Paul said, "By grace you have been saved through faith, and this is not your doing; it is the gift of God" (Eph 2:8–9). We don't have to remain "as we are." That's the good news! We can be better. We can do more. We can change. Jacob is an excellent example of a drastic conversion.

Finally, we've learned that if we begin to adjust our attitudes and alter our behavior, we will become more and more Christlike. Paul said, "I am confident of this, that the one who began a good work in you will continue to complete it" (Phil 1:6).

We must also realize that conversion or change may not be an instantaneous event. All of us are "under construction." Christians "grow in grace." Even Jesus grew: "The child grew and became strong, filled with wisdom, and the favor of God was upon him" (Luke 2:40).

Peter urged us to "Grow in the grace and knowledge of our Lord and Savior Jesus Christ" (2 Pet 3:18).

These are powerful lessons. Applying them in our lives every day makes the scripture real and allows God's word to speak to us.

6.

Of Coats and Forgiveness

Every child knows the story of Joseph and his coat of many colors. The scriptures say,

> Joseph, being seventeen years old, was shepherding the flock with his brothers.… Now Israel loved Joseph more than any other of his children because he was the son of his old age, and he made him an ornamented robe. But when his brothers saw that their father loved him more than all his brothers, they hated him and could not speak peaceably to him.… They conspired to kill him. They said to one another, "Here comes this dreamer. Come now, let us kill him and throw him into one of the pits; then we shall say that a wild animal has devoured him, and we shall see what will become of his dreams." But when Reuben heard it, he delivered him out of their hands, saying, "Let us not take his life." Reuben said to them, "Shed no blood; throw him into this pit here in the wilderness, but lay no hand on him"—that he might rescue him out of their hand and restore him to his father. So when Joseph came to his brothers, they stripped him of his robe, the ornamented robe that he wore, and they took him and threw him into a pit.… When some Midianite traders passed by, they drew Joseph up, lifting him out of the pit, and sold him to the Ishmaelites for twenty pieces of silver. And they took Joseph to Egypt. (Gen 37:2–4, 18–24, 28)

Joseph was sold and spent many years in exile. He was falsely accused and imprisoned, but because of his faith and insight, he became a ruler in Egypt.

Then a great drought brought his brothers to Egypt searching for food. They didn't recognize Joseph, but when he revealed himself to his brothers, they remembered what they did to him and were afraid. But he forgave them for their treachery: "'I am your brother, Joseph, whom you sold into Egypt. And now do not be distressed or angry with yourselves because you sold me here, for God sent me before you to preserve life.'... And he kissed all his brothers and wept upon them.... 'Even though you intended to do harm to me, God intended it for good, in order to preserve a numerous people, as he is doing today. So have no fear; I myself will provide for you and your little ones.' In this way he reassured them, speaking kindly to them" (Gen 45:4–5, 15; 50:20–21).

Now, what is the purpose of this passage? What deeper meaning is it trying to express? Most importantly, how can it speak to us today?

Well, we still wear coats, families still show favoritism, and sibling rivalry is still common. Furthermore, pride still makes relationships difficult to maintain. Bitterness is still a dangerous element that causes conflict between people. Therefore, it's obvious that one of the main purposes of this story is to emphasize the necessity of forgiveness.

Most of us, like Joseph, tend to be proud of certain possessions. We tend to be arrogant about special privileges. Firstborn children may try to control younger siblings. Favorite children may use their status to their advantage. This attitude causes family conflict. It feeds envy and jealousy and often leads to violence.

Such pride is destructive. An old fable tells that Satan was observing a group of little demons who were tempting an elderly saint. They tested him with all the sins of the flesh but failed. They tried to fill his mind with doubts and fears, but again they failed.

Then Satan said, "Your methods are too crude. This is what I recommend." Going up to the saint, he slyly asked, "Have you heard the news? Your brother has just been chosen as bishop instead of you." The fable says that immediately jealousy and envy overcame the old man.

Few of us are beyond such insecurity and conceit. Also, we usually feel that it's our status and possessions that make us great. But Joseph's coat didn't make him great; the trials and tribulations did.

When a woman asked Jesus to give her sons a special position of importance, Jesus refused. The scriptures say, "The mother of the sons of Zebedee came to him with her sons, and kneeling before him, she asked a favor of him.... 'Declare that these two sons of mine will sit, one at your right hand

and one at your left, in your kingdom.' But Jesus answered, 'You do not know what you are asking. Are you able to drink the cup that I am about to drink?' They said to him, 'We are able.' He said to them, 'You will indeed drink my cup, but to sit at my right hand and at my left, this is not mine to grant'" (see Matt 20:20–23).

Greatness cannot be given. Jacob couldn't give it to Joseph. He had to earn it! There's a vast difference between the Joseph who was sold into Egypt and the Joseph who provided grain for his brothers. At first he interpreted his dreams to mean he was so wonderful and grand that even nature worshiped him. In the scripture he says, "The sun, the moon, and eleven stars were bowing down to me'" (see Gen 37:9–10).

Later he took no credit at all for his wisdom: "Pharaoh said to Joseph, 'I had a dream, and there is no one who can interpret it. I have heard it said of you that when you hear a dream you can interpret it.' Joseph answered Pharaoh, 'It is not I; God will give Pharaoh a favorable answer'" (Gen 41:15–16).

He had finally learned humility. At first he was interested in receiving praise and honor. Later he was interested in serving others. At first he was angry and resentful at what had happened to him. Later he was forgiving and grateful that it had been a blessing in disguise, saying, "'Do not be distressed or angry with yourselves because you sold me here, for God sent me before you to preserve life.'… Then his brothers also wept, fell down before him, and said, 'We are here as your slaves.' But Joseph said to them, 'Do not be afraid! Am I in the place of God? Even though you intended to do harm to me, God intended it for good, in order to preserve a numerous people, as he is doing today'" (see Gen 45:5; 50:18–20).

So what should we do about envious attitudes, jealous feelings, and refusals to offer forgiveness? We must examine ourselves. What makes you arrogant? Are you vain about your appearance? Your clothes? Your car? Do you look down on those with less? Are you conceited about your achievements? Your knowledge? Your worldly experiences? Do you treat those who are ignorant and inexperienced with disdain? Are you self-righteous about your morality? Do you despise those who have slipped or sinned in certain areas?

Now, we should realize that Joseph had ample reasons to be proud. His arrogance wasn't based on ill-founded illusions. He was an unusually gifted and intelligent young man. The dreams were indications of his future. In fact, those dreams actually came true, and the whole family did eventually bow before him.

His problem wasn't that he was an empty boaster. His problem was that he handled his abilities and possibilities in an inappropriate way. True spirituality makes us humble and altruistic.

In the story of Joseph, there is not just one villain. Instead, there's enough blame to go around. Almost every character added to the problem. Jacob was not a wise father. He should not have shown favoritism among his children. Every child deserves an equal share of his parents' love and resources.

Joseph was not humble. He should not have boasted and bragged about his special status. No one likes to be humiliated and told they are inferior. If we're mature and self-confident, we don't need to put others down.

Even so, the brothers certainly should not have reacted with hatred and violence. Nevertheless, this story is relevant and realistic. People and families make these same mistakes every day. Like us, all of these characters learned lessons and had to live with the consequences of their mistakes. Jacob suffered years of grief and regret, believing his son was dead. Joseph went through decades of hardships. He experienced unfair attacks and spent time in prison. These things helped him develop his character and strengthen his faith.

The psalmist expressed it this way: "Before I was humbled I went astray, but now I keep your word.... It is good for me that I was humbled, so that I might learn your statutes" (Ps 119:67, 71).

Paul agreed, saying, "We…boast in our afflictions, knowing that affliction produces endurance, and endurance produces character, and character produces hope" (Rom 5:3–4).

Now, what have we learned from this account of Joseph and his coat? Unfortunately, the only thing most people know about Joseph is that he wore a fancy, colorful garment. If that's all we know, we've totally missed God's word to us.

Remember, Paul said, "Scripture is inspired by God and is useful for teaching" (2 Tim 3:16).

To make this scripture useful in our lives, we must discover and apply the deeper moral teachings. We must get beyond the literal words to the meaning.

First, we've seen that jealousy and envy are very destructive attitudes. They destroy families, businesses, churches, and nations. James said, "Where there is envy and selfish ambition, there will also be disorder and wickedness of every kind" (Jas 3:16).

Jesus spent much of his time discussing how to have good relationships. He emphasized peace and unity. Discord and contention cause chaos in society. They were even evident among the twelve apostles.

Next, we've realized that forgiveness is the crucial element in a Christian's life. God forgave us. We must forgive others. Paul said, "Be kind to one another, tenderhearted, forgiving one another, as God in Christ has forgiven you" (Eph 4:32).

Holding on to anger and hostility causes most personal and social problems. Bitterness is a deadly emotion. It makes a person physically and mentally ill. It causes people to consider revenge, and this often results in violence and crime.

Finally, we've been able to understand that with faith and determination, even tragic experiences can be used for good. Joseph illustrates the scripture that says, "We know that all things work together for good for those who love God, who are called according to his purpose" (Rom 8:28).

One of the most encouraging and hopeful teachings of Jesus is that all our experiences, both good and evil, can actually be used productively. God can salvage wasted actions and turn bad decisions into learning experiences. Realizing that even our sins and errors can be useful gives us hope.

These are powerful lessons. Applying them in our lives every day makes this scripture real and allows God's word to speak to us.

7.

Of Burning Bushes and Commitment

After Joseph died, the Egyptians became suspicious of the Hebrews. Pharaoh ordered every Jewish baby boy to be cast into the river. The scripture says,

> Now a man from the house of Levi went and married a Levite woman. The woman conceived and bore a son, and when she saw that he was a fine baby, she hid him three months. When she could hide him no longer she got a papyrus basket for him and plastered it with bitumen and pitch; she put the child in it and placed it among the reeds on the bank of the river. His sister stood at a distance, to see what would happen to him. The daughter of Pharaoh came down to bathe at the river, while her attendants walked beside the river. She saw the basket among the reeds and sent her maid to bring it. When she opened it, she saw the child. He was crying, and she took pity on him. "This must be one of the Hebrews' children," she said. Then his sister said to Pharaoh's daughter, "Shall I go and get you a nurse from the Hebrew women to nurse the child for you?" Pharaoh's daughter said to her, "Yes." So the girl went and called the child's mother. Pharaoh's daughter said to her, "Take this child and nurse it for me, and I will give you your wages." So the woman took the child and nursed it. When the child grew up, she brought him to Pharaoh's daughter, and he became her son. She named him Moses, "because," she said, "I drew him out of the water." (Exod 2:1–10)

Moses grew up in the royal family. However, one day he murdered an Egyptian for mistreating a Hebrew slave and had to leave Egypt. The scripture says,

> Moses was keeping the flock of his father-in-law Jethro, the priest of Midian; he led his flock beyond the wilderness and came to Mount Horeb, the mountain of God. There the angel of the LORD appeared to him in a flame of fire out of a bush; he looked, and the bush was blazing, yet it was not consumed. Then Moses said, "I must turn aside and look at this great sight and see why the bush is not burned up." When the LORD saw that he had turned aside to see, God called to him out of the bush, "Moses, Moses!" And he said, "Here I am." Then he said, "Come no closer! Remove the sandals from your feet, for the place on which you are standing is holy ground." (Exod 3:1–5)

Now, why was this particular spot holy ground? Well, it was at this place that God gave Moses the mission of leading his people to freedom. He became one of the few truly great men of history. This story shows us that any place becomes holy ground if it's where we feel the presence of God, receive a message from God, or make a personal commitment to God.

Paul said, "Do you not know that you are God's temple and that God's Spirit dwells in you?... For God's temple is holy, and you are that temple" (1 Cor 3:16–17).

In the Old Testament the people tended to place God on mountains or in temples. They revered the ark of the covenant and other sacred objects. Today we still think of God as being associated with the church, the Bible, or a cross. But concrete reminders aren't as important as spiritual experiences.

John Wesley, the founder of Methodism, was counseling a woman who had left a life of prostitution to follow Christ. She asked what she could do with her limited abilities. The minister said, "Tell others what you have found."

"What have I found?" she asked.

"You have found that God knows your name," the wise man replied.

Yes, God called Moses by name, and he knows our names too. Our God is great enough to specialize in individuals. When Julia Ward Howe wrote to a senator on behalf of a poor man, the senator excused himself, saying he was too busy with the affairs of the nation to take time for individuals. Her answer was, "When last I heard, God had not developed this attitude."

In his parables Jesus did not speak of lost flocks but of one lost sheep. All encounters with God involve individuals. He touches each of us at our point of need.

It's significant that God has chosen to call Himself "I AM." He does not say, "I am your creator" or "I am your light." He simply says, "I AM!" It's as if he is saying, "Are you weak? I am strength! Are you poor? I am wealth! Are you troubled? I am comfort! Are you sick? I am health! Are you dying? I am life! Whatever is desirable or needful, that is what 'I AM.'"

This encounter with Moses teaches us that God is both holy and personal. But it's a two-way covenant. When he calls us to a mission, we must commit to his will. Henry Ward Beecher, the great minister, once said, "If the architect of a house had one plan and the contractor had another, what conflicts would there be? How many walls would have to come down? How many doors and windows would need to be altered before the two could harmonize!" When it comes to the building of life, God is the architect, and men and women are the contractors. God has one plan, but too often we have another. That explains the problems and tragedies around us.

If the contractor doesn't follow the architect's plans, chaos is inevitable. Musicians sometimes perform music that contains dissonance. When you hear two notes that clash, you say, "Oh, that hurts." But when that chord resolves into perfect harmony, you say, "Ah, that's nice." One man said, "At our house, if you're standing in the hallway, you'll often have a good example of dissonance and discord. I usually have classical music playing in my bedroom. But something very different may be coming from my teenager's bedroom. As long as you're in one or the other of the bedrooms, you're okay, but if you stand between the two, you're going to get noise. I guarantee it."

Our life is like that. We have discord when we allow ourselves to be pulled in opposite directions at once. Moses received a clear call to action. It was up to him to carry it out.

Have you seen a burning bush? Where is your holy ground? Are there special places or experiences that inspire you? One man described a moment of worship this way: "At a certain point during a service, I may feel connected to God. And I think, 'Of course! This is it! We're all part of something wonderful! We're all united in love!' And then that epiphany begins to fade away. If we had it all the time, we'd take it for granted. But having it come back again and again touches our heart and soul. We know there is this place of sacredness."

Most of us have such a holy place. We know that's where we ought to be. Each time we get lost in paralyzing doubts, in hostile thoughts, and in judgmental attitudes, a little voice deep inside reminds us of that place. Music, nature, and worship experiences can provide such spiritual connections. We desperately need these moments.

When Moses met with God by the burning bush, he was commanded to take off his shoes, for he was standing in a holy place. What was so sacred about the backside of a desert mountain? Surely it was not just because God was there. God is omnipresent! It could not have been because Moses himself was especially holy. He had just murdered a man. No, that was a holy place because it represented a man's encounter with God. Moses discovered that he didn't need a temple or an altar to be in a holy place. God came to him while he was doing his daily chores. Our home, our office, or our factory becomes holy if we encounter the presence of God there.

Now, what have we learned from this account of Moses and the burning bush? Unfortunately, the only thing most people know about this story is that a man saw a fire in the desert. If that's all we know, we've totally missed God's word to us.

Remember, Paul said, "Scripture is inspired by God and is useful for teaching" (2 Tim 3:16).

To make this scripture useful in our lives, we must discover and apply the deeper moral teachings. We must get beyond the literal words to the meaning.

First, we've learned that wherever God meets a man or a woman, that is holy ground. Paul said, "Do you not know that your body is a temple of the Holy Spirit within you, which you have from God?" (1 Cor 6:19). The realization that "holiness" is not limited to certain objects or locations changes our outlook. God isn't "out there" or "up there." He is "in here." He is with us wherever we are. This scripture shows that a burning bush in the wilderness can be just as sacred as a temple or an altar or a stained-glass window.

Next, we've learned that God has a message, a plan, and a purpose for every individual. He says, "I know the plans I have for you…plans for your welfare and not for harm, to give you a future with hope" (Jer 29:11). This is one of the most significant principles of Christianity. Knowing that God has a special plan and purpose for your life is a mind-blowing, life-changing idea. Moses was called by name, and so are we.

Finally, we've learned that each of us must meet God in a holy moment of connection. Each of us must make a total commitment to his will. Each of us must experience a personal call to service. Then, when he calls us, each of our responses must be like that of Simon and Andrew. The scripture says, "As Jesus passed along the Sea of Galilee, he saw Simon and his brother Andrew casting a net into the sea, for they were fishermen. And Jesus said to them, 'Follow me, and I will make you fishers of people.' And immediately they left their nets and followed him" (Mark 1:16–18).

Such a divine invitation determines our destiny. Do we hear and understand? Do we consider the mission as a blessing and an opportunity? Do we take our responsibility in the matter seriously? Such crucial questions will define our lives.

These are powerful lessons. Applying them in our lives every day makes the scripture real and allows God's word to speak to us.

8.

Of Seas and Progress

Many stories and movies have dealt with the parting of the Red Sea. When Moses led the Israelites out of slavery in Egypt, they immediately encountered a seemingly insurmountable obstacle. There was a body of water ahead of them and a threatening army behind them. The scripture says,

> The Egyptians pursued them, all Pharaoh's horses and chariots, his chariot drivers and his army; they overtook them.... As Pharaoh drew near…in great fear the Israelites called out to the LORD.... Moses said to the people, "Do not be afraid, stand firm, and see the deliverance that the LORD will accomplish for you today, for the Egyptians whom you see today you shall never see again. The LORD will fight for you."… The LORD said to Moses, "Why do you cry out to me? Tell the Israelites to go forward. But you lift up your staff and stretch out your hand over the sea and divide it, that the Israelites may go into the sea on dry ground.... The Egyptians…will go in after them.... The Egyptians shall know that I am the LORD.... Then Moses stretched out his hand over the sea. The LORD drove the sea back by a strong east wind all night and turned the sea into dry land, and the waters were divided. The Israelites went into the sea on dry ground, the waters forming a wall for them on their right and on their left. The Egyptians pursued and went into the sea after them, all of Pharaoh's horses, chariots, and chariot drivers. (Exod 14:9, 10, 13–14, 15–16, 17, 18, 21–23)

Now, what is the purpose of this passage? What deeper meaning is it trying to express? Most importantly, how can it speak to us today?

Well, our physical paths probably won't be blocked by a sea. Besides, we have ferries, ships, and even hovercrafts to get past water barriers now. Therefore, in order to benefit from this scripture, we must use it as an analogy for our problems. It's obvious that the purpose of this story is to teach us an important lesson about how to overcome obstacles and make progress.

Almost all of us will eventually come to a "Red Sea" in our lives. At such times, regression is impossible, and stalling is deadly. Our only option is to go forward through the difficulty.

It can be difficult to go through illnesses, depressions, sorrows, and tragedies, but it's the only way. Going back or standing still is impossible. As with the Israelites, "going forward" into a threatening sea is frightening. It requires determination. It's significant that these Israelites' dilemma wasn't solved before they proceeded. Instead, it was only after they actually took the first step into the midst of the sea that a way through was provided.

It's also significant that God said, "Don't just stand there and complain. Don't just beg for a miracle. Don't continue to wait for perfect circumstances. Dare to move out in faith!"

There's a time to pray and a time to act. This was a time to act. The principle is this: When we put forth effort, obstacles will diminish. We can't wait until everything is right before we move. Sometimes the only way to overcome an impediment is simply to do the very thing we fear most.

Those who demand a guarantee of success before they try will never even begin, much less finish, any worthwhile task.

A visitor once asked an old farmer, "How's your cotton?"

"Didn't plant no cotton; 'feer'd of the boll weevil."

"How are your potatoes?"

"Didn't plant no 'taters; 'feer'd of the 'tater bugs."

"How is your corn?"

"Didn't plant no corn; 'feer'd of the crows."

"Well, what did you plant?"

"Didn't plant nuthin'—jest playin' it safe."

There's an old saying: "Nothing risked, nothing gained." Also, opportunities often come disguised as problems. When his parishioners complained to an old preacher about their misfortunes, he would always say, "Congratulations! The more problems you have, the more possibilities you have."

A traveler in the Swiss Alps spent the night with his guide in a chalet high up in the mountains. Early the next morning he was awakened by terrific crashing and rumblings. Frightened, he aroused his guide and asked, "What's happening? Is the world coming to an end?"

Calmly, the guide answered, "No! You see, when the sun comes up, its rays touch the snow at the peak, causing it to hurtle down into the valley. Then the ice begins to crack. This loud racket is not the end of the world; it's only the dawn of a new day."

Life is like that. Experiences that seem like the end can really be the beginning. What looked like the end of the world was the dawn of a new day for these Hebrews. What looked like a tragic defeat was really a great victory.

A perceptive poet wrote:

> When you come to that Red Sea place in your life
> And your enemies try to pursue,
> You must quickly go forward with courage and faith.
> That's what every Christian must do.

So what sea has parted for you? What obstacles have you overcome? Have you ever faced an impasse with no solution in sight? Have you ever encountered a barrier that seemed to be insurmountable? Have you ever been stymied by circumstances? Have you ever been cornered with no way to escape? Have you ever ended up on a dead-end street?

In short, what should we do when we have problems? What should we do when seemingly impossible obstructions block our path to success?

We're paralyzed by fear and indecision. It takes faith and courage to make progress. Furthermore, sometimes we must go forward before we're assured of success, and that's hard to do. Suppose a baby were to say, "My legs are so small and weak that there's no use to start kicking yet. I'll wait until they grow big and strong"? What would happen to that baby's legs? They would stay weak. They would never grow strong until he used them.

It's the same with us. Sometimes we must move before the path is clear. That's the only way to overcome obstacles. Giving up is never the answer. These Israelites had to move in order to reach the promised land, and so do we.

We must have confidence in our own abilities. Paul said, "I can do all things through him who strengthens me" (Phil 4:13).

Years ago, a baseball team lost seventeen of their first twenty games. It just so happened that a famous magician was attracting a lot of attention in the area. Some people thought he could perform miracles.

One afternoon, the manager took all the bats and left for a few hours. When he returned, he told his team the magician had put a powerful spell on their bats and promised that if they used these bats, they would win the game.

The following day, the team got thirty-seven hits and twenty runs. From that day on, they couldn't be beat.

Of course, nothing had happened to those bats. Instead, something had happened in the minds of those ball players! Confidence led to success. Confidence always leads to success because confidence means "with faith"!

Now, what have we learned from this account about the parting of the Red Sea? Unfortunately, when they consider the fleeing Hebrews, most people merely visualize the movie scene of Moses raising his staff over the water. If that's all we know, we've totally missed God's word to us.

Remember, Paul said, "Scripture is inspired by God and is useful for teaching" (2 Tim 3:16).

To make this scripture useful in our lives, we must discover and apply the deeper moral teachings. We must get beyond the literal words to the meaning.

First, we need to be absolutely certain we're on the path God has planned for us. The scripture said, "God did not lead them by way of the land of the Philistines, although that was nearer, for God thought, 'If the people face war, they may change their minds and return to Egypt.' So God led the people by the roundabout way of the wilderness bordering the Red Sea" (Exod 13:17–18).

Sometimes the fastest way is not the best way!

Men and women must decide how they will live out their allotted time on this earth. All of us have free will to choose our lifestyle. Will it be positive or negative? Will it be useful or useless? Will it make the world better or worse? Finding God's will concerning our mate, our career, and our lifestyle—and then obeying that will—is our responsibility.

Next, we need to realize that God uses ordinary life events to answer our prayers. In the case of Moses and the Red Sea, God didn't wave a magic wand. He used a natural resource. He used the wind. Furthermore, this wasn't an instantaneous act. As with most solutions, it took time. The scripture says, "The LORD drove the sea back by a strong east wind all night and turned the sea into dry land, and the waters were divided" (Exod 14:21).

Some people expect supernatural guidance. They wait for overt signs and special omens to show them what to do and where to go. This seldom happens. Instead, God usually uses normal people and regular events to lead each of us.

Finally, we need to make the first step of faith instead of waiting for a quick fix or a miraculous intervention. When Moses and the Israelites hesitated,

"The LORD said to Moses, 'Why do you cry out to me? Tell the Israelites to go forward'" (Exod 14:15).

Until they took the first step, nothing happened. We are made to move. God created us to exert our own energy in order to make progress.

These are powerful lessons. Applying them in our lives every day makes this scripture real and allows God's word to speak to us.

9.

Of Walls and Success

Joshua and the walls of Jericho are well known in both songs and stories. The scripture says,

> Now Jericho was shut up inside and out because of the Israelites; no one came out, and no one went in. The LORD said to Joshua, "See, I have handed Jericho over to you, along with its king and soldiers. You shall march around the city, all the warriors circling the city once. Thus you shall do for six days, with seven priests bearing seven trumpets of rams' horns before the ark. On the seventh day you shall march around the city seven times, the priests blowing the trumpets. When they make a long blast with the ram's horn, as soon as you hear the sound of the trumpet, then all the people shall shout with a great shout, and the wall of the city will fall down flat, and all the people shall charge straight ahead."… As Joshua had commanded the people, the seven priests carrying the seven trumpets of rams' horns before the LORD went forward, blowing the trumpets, with the ark of the covenant of the LORD following them. And the armed men went before the priests who blew the trumpets; the rear guard came after the ark, while the trumpets blew continually…. On the second day they marched around the city once and then returned to the camp. They did this for six days. On the seventh day they rose early, at dawn, and marched around the city in the same manner seven times. It was only on that day that they marched around the city seven times. And at the seventh time, when the priests had blown the trumpets,

Joshua said to the people, "Shout! For the LORD has given you the city." (Josh 6:1–5, 8–9, 14–16)

Now, what is the purpose of this passage? What deeper meaning is it trying to express? Most importantly, how can it speak to us today?

Well, modern cities are not usually protected by walls. Furthermore, our armies use missiles and drones rather than trumpets and horns. Even so, we can learn much about life from this scripture. It's obvious that the purpose of this dramatic story is to teach us an important lesson about how to achieve success.

Like the Hebrews under Joshua's command, when things are going well, we often assume that our hardships are behind us forever. But in this case victory was not assured, and success would not be easily accomplished. The land was already well populated. Its cities were crowded with Canaanites, and the city-states were fortified. Jericho, with its massive walls, was the obstacle that blocked their success. It was the spies, aided by Rahab, along with the psychological warfare of trumpets and shouts, that caused the walls of Jericho to come tumbling down.

Sometimes we come up against such formidable walls. At that point we can simply give up, or we can stand there and beat our heads against the stones, or we can use our initiative and cause those barriers to crumble before our very eyes.

Top performers in any field get to the top by confronting the things they fear. A boxing trainer once told his student, "Winners and cowards feel exactly the same anxiety. Winners just react to it differently."

Having a positive outlook is important. Research shows that imaging something in the mind fires the nervous system the same way as actually doing it. Also, the imaging must be positive. That means if a golfer tells himself, "Don't hit the ball into the water," his mind immediately sees the image of the ball going into the water. Therefore, that's where the ball is likely to land! Before dealing with any difficult situation, focus only on what you hope will happen, not on the disaster you're afraid might happen.

A ski instructor said, "I learned the value of taking small steps when I trained some novices on a difficult slope. Going to the edge of the run, they would look all the way down to the bottom. Invariably, the hill would seem too steep and too difficult, and they'd back away. To help them overcome their fears, I would tell them not to think of skiing the whole hill, instead trying to make it to the first turn. This changed their focus. Now they were looking at what they could do, rather than at what they couldn't do."

Overcoming begins with an attitude of confidence and faith. Jesus said, "I have said this to you so that in me you may have peace. In the world you face persecution, but take courage: I have conquered the world!" (John 16:33).

John said, "Whatever is born of God conquers the world. And this is the victory that conquers the world, our faith" (1 John 5:4).

God says, "Those who conquer will inherit these things, and I will be their God, and they will be my children" (Rev 21:7).

Joshua believed they could overcome. He had faith the task could be done. This enabled them to do it. An anonymous poet wrote:

> The man who misses all the fun
> > Is he who says, "It can't be done."
> > In solemn pride, he stands aloof
> > And greets each venture with reproof.
> Had he the power, he would efface
> > The history of the human race.
> > We'd have no radio, no cars,
> > No airplanes, and no manmade stars,
> No telegraph, no telephone.
> > We'd wander in the dark alone.
> > The world would sleep if things were run
> > By folks who say, "It can't be done."

So how can we tear down walls? How can we overcome barriers? How can we achieve success in life? This story about Joshua and the walls of Jericho gives us some answers.

Overcoming requires a lot of planning and preparation. Robert Schuller said, "Failures are divided into two classes: Those who thought and never did, and those who did and never thought. Winners, on the other hand, do both." We must think through our challenges and then take decisive action. We must learn from the past and anticipate the future. Most importantly, we must have confidence in ourselves and faith in God. Overcoming requires motivation and determination.

Furthermore, we can't wait until things get easy. George Washington met a wall when he crossed the Delaware to attack Trenton. He was greatly outnumbered, and a third of the soldiers he did have were too ill to fight, but he decided to attack anyway. In his journal he wrote: My men "were without shoes or stockings.... They were without any proper shirts or waistcoats.... They were also in great (need) of blankets." A blizzard came, followed by freezing rain, but Washington pressed on. When his soldiers' muskets got wet and wouldn't fire, he led a bayonet charge. After the battle, over thirty of the enemy were dead and nine hundred were taken prisoners. Only four Americans had been wounded. Washington knew if he waited for good health, fine clothes, warm weather, a full stomach, and ammunition, the war would be lost.

It's the same with us. Christians must take God's promise seriously when he said, "My grace is sufficient for you, for power is made perfect in weakness" (2 Cor 12:9).

Overcoming includes patience and persistence. When you are tempted to abandon a job because it looks impossible, think of the bee! A bee has to visit fifty-six thousand red clover blossoms in order to gather enough nectar to make one pound of honey! The task seems impossible, but they do it anyway.

Above all, overcoming means reaching the goal and completing the task! You can't stop short. An energetic employee asked his boss, "How can I have a successful life?" His boss answered, "When you start a thing, finish it!"

Are you an overcomer, or do you expect defeat? Do you have fears and anxieties that are holding you back? Do you have guilt and regrets that are occupying your mind? Do you have resentments that are sapping your strength? What is hindering you from being happy, productive, and fulfilled? In short, what walls are separating you from success? These are important questions.

Now, what have we learned from this account of Joshua and the walls of Jericho? Unfortunately, the only thing most people know about the matter is that the song says, "Joshua fought the battle of Jericho, and the walls came tumbling down." If that's all we know, we've totally missed God's word to us.

Remember, Paul said, "Scripture is inspired by God and is useful for teaching" (2 Tim 3:16).

To make this scripture useful in our lives, we must discover and apply the deeper moral teachings. We must get beyond the literal words to the meaning.

First, we've learned that breaking down walls of resistance requires a lot of plans, preparations, and just plain work. Nothing simply happens! James says, "Be doers of the word and not merely hearers who deceive themselves" (Jas 1:22). Inertia is a deadly habit. Letting things slide never leads to success. Gardens don't weed themselves. Houses don't build themselves. Little elves don't come in to do our chores every night. Dreams, plans, and hopes are nice, but at some point we must act.

Next, we've learned that breaking down walls of resistance requires patience. Most achievements that are worthwhile take time. Being willing to wait and defer gratification is an important trait. Paul says, "If we hope for what we do not see, we wait for it with patience" (Rom 8:25). Most of us are impatient. We want something, and we want it now! But that seldom happens. We can't plant a seed this morning and expect roses by sundown. The results of our efforts are rarely revealed instantaneously.

Finally, we've learned that breaking down walls of resistance requires perseverance. The walls of Jericho didn't fall overnight. They didn't fall the first time they marched around the city. Instead, it took seven days, and on the seventh day they had to march around the city seven times before they were successful.

Now, in the Hebrew culture the number seven meant "completion." This means we must keep on keeping on for as long as it takes to achieve success. We must not give up. If at first you don't succeed, try, try again. Paul says, "Let us not grow weary in doing what is right, for we will reap at harvest time, if we do not give up" (Gal 6:9).

Difficult tasks require persistence. We can't just knock once on a door and expect to receive a response. Sometimes we must knock repeatedly. One lesson doesn't make you a concert pianist. One day of skiing doesn't make you an Olympic champion. One victorious battle doesn't win a war. Practice makes perfect. Edison had thousands of failures with his light bulb before he achieved success.

These are powerful lessons. Applying them in our lives every day makes this scripture real and allows God's word to speak to us.

10.

Of Giants and Service

The contest between David and Goliath is probably the most popular story in the Bible. Everybody has heard about that!

David visited his brothers, who were soldiers. But Saul's whole army was helpless before the giant, Goliath.

> David said to Saul, "Let no one's heart fail because of him; your servant will go and fight with this Philistine." Saul said to David, "You are not able to go against this Philistine to fight with him, for you are just a boy, and he has been a warrior from his youth." But David said to Saul, "Your servant used to keep sheep for his father, and whenever a lion or a bear came and took a lamb from the flock, I went after it and struck it down, rescuing the lamb from its mouth, and if it turned against me, I would catch it by the jaw, strike it down, and kill it. Your servant has killed both lions and bears, and this uncircumcised Philistine shall be like one of them, since he has defied the armies of the living God." David said, "The LORD, who saved me from the paw of the lion and from the paw of the bear, will save me from the hand of this Philistine." So Saul said to David, "Go, and may the LORD be with you!"… He put a bronze helmet on [David's] head and clothed him with a coat of mail. David strapped Saul's sword over the armor, and he tried in vain to walk, for he was not used to them. Then David said to Saul, "I cannot walk with these, for I am not used to them." So David removed them. Then he took his staff in his hand and chose five smooth stones from the wadi and put them in his shepherd's bag, in

the pouch; his sling was in his hand, and he drew near to the Philistine.... When the Philistine drew nearer to meet David, David...took out a stone, slung it, and struck the Philistine on his forehead; the stone sank into his forehead, and he fell face down on the ground. (1 Sam 17:32–37, 38–40, 48–49)

Now, what is the purpose of this passage? What deeper meaning is it trying to express? Most importantly, how can it speak to us today?

Well, I doubt any of us will meet an eight-foot-tall giant this week, and we probably don't even own a slingshot, so David's wonderful and courageous deed can't be applied to our lives in a literal sense. However, there are many valuable lessons about service to be gained from this story.

Sooner or later, each of us will meet a giant. When that happens, we have a choice. We can make excuses and walk away. Or, like David, we can view it as our call, accept the challenge, and confront it head-on.

In making this decision the pessimist sees the disadvantages, and the optimist sees the advantages. When Goliath encountered the Israelites, the soldiers all thought, "He's so big; we can't kill him." But David looked at the giant and thought, "He's so big; I can't miss him!"

When David chose to confront the giant, the king offered his own recommendations and resources, but the wise young man refused, saying, "I must use my own weapons to slay my giant." It's the same with us. Facing adversity is a personal thing. The king tried to persuade David to use his armor, his helmet, and his sword. These objects represent reliance on tradition, authority, and external forces. They won't work!

Even well-meaning advice and offers of help may be more of a liability than an asset. Each of us is uniquely equipped for service. Therefore, we must use our own internal resources to solve our problems.

So what were David's resources? David had responsibility. He didn't say, "Someone should do something." He said, "I can do something."

Once, after a decisive confrontation, Napoleon awarded each of his soldiers a simple medal. It was inscribed with the name of the battlefield and the phrase "I was there." Both officers and enlisted men received the same honor. Regardless of rank, everyone was proud of their badge.

Someday we shall all give an account of what we did in this life. Will we say, "I was there; I was in the battle"? We may not always win, but there's something worse than losing, and that's having to say, "I never even tried." David knew it only takes one person to make a difference in the course of history.

David also had confidence. He believed in himself. He had past experiences of success when his sheep were attacked by wild animals. He had always come through in a crunch. He had faced other crises, and he could face this one.

David had courage. We don't know what we can do until we try. In an experiment at an aquarium, a savage barracuda attempted to attack a mackerel but was stopped by a glass partition in the tank. After repeatedly bumping his nose, he finally quit trying. Eventually, the partition was removed, but the barracuda still stopped at the point where the barrier had been. He thought it was still there! The invisible obstruction was as effective as a real one.

Many of us are like that. We move forward until we reach an imaginary barrier. Then we stop because of a self-imposed attitude of limitation. Courage overcomes limitations. In fact, adversity often brings out unexpected courage.

In the dry northern Rockies, fire has been a critical threat from primitive times. However, the lodgepole pine, the region's dominant evergreen, produces a cone that remains on the tree for decades. The only thing that causes the cones to drop and release their seeds is heat. So when the forests burn, the blaze that consumes the mature trees triggers the release of seeds that would otherwise remain dormant. Like that pine, we as human beings carry seeds of undeveloped potential that are released only in the heat of adversity.

David had such potential.

So what does this story teach us about service? What giants have you confronted? What do you do in a crisis? Well, our giant may not be named Goliath, but it can be just as formidable and deadly. Our giant may be a moral dilemma. It may be a choice of lifestyle. It may be a career decision.

The giant we need to confront may be our own pride, hostility, or greed, but more than likely our giant is fear and procrastination. In short, there comes a time in all our lives when we just have to act! No more questions, no more hesitation, no more counting the cost. When you meet your giant, it's time for action!

Historians say Michelangelo wrestled with himself, trying to decide how to depict the figure in his massive statue of David. At last he decided to show David at the moment of his decision to fight rather than at the later moment of victory. When a friend asked why he chose that particular position, he answered, "Because the thing that made David great was not his killing of Goliath. It was his decision of commitment." Decision is more important than execution, because if the decision is right, the execution invariably follows. The moment David declared, "I will go and fight," victory was assured.

It's the same with us. There's something about a courageous decision. It enables and motivates us. It moves us past the point of no return. It commits us to a plan of action.

The shepherd boy David faced a dangerous enemy. He refused the king's offer of aid because it didn't fit him. Instead, he killed the giant, Goliath, with his slingshot.

The most significant characteristic about David is his desire to serve. David was willing to meet this challenge because he knew projects are not to be evaluated in terms of the probability of success, but rather in terms of the value of the goal. David knew the odds, but he also knew it was worth it, and he was willing to try.

David had faith. Faith involves risk. That's why we say "leap of faith." It's like the trapeze artists in the circus. They swing back and forth hanging on to the trapeze bar, but if that's all they did, there would be no thrill for the audience. It's that split second when the artist lets go of the bar and is flying through the air with the greatest of ease that makes the audience stand up and cheer. It's the letting go and trusting that the other trapeze will arrive at just the right moment that gives life meaning and excitement.

David's confrontation with Goliath was such a moment.

Now, what have we learned from this account of David and Goliath? Unfortunately, the only thing most people know about the story is that David killed a giant with one stone. If that's all we know, we've totally missed God's word to us.

Remember Paul said, "Scripture is inspired by God and is useful for teaching" (2 Tim 3:16).

To make this scripture useful in our lives, we must discover and apply the deeper moral teachings. We must get beyond the literal words to the meaning.

So what practical principles have we learned? First, we've learned that one person can make a difference. David did what an army could not do. We won't be judged by what everyone else does. We'll be judged by what we do. Paul said, "Each one of us will be held accountable" (Rom 14:12).

It's exciting to discover that my small contributions are important in this world. One vote can make a difference. I have skills no one else has. I can do things no one else can do. I can influence people no one else can influence. I am an essential piece of life's jigsaw puzzle.

Next, we've learned that each of us must use our own talents, skills, and resources and never try to imitate other people. David couldn't use the king's armor and sword. He had to use his own talents and abilities. Peter says, "Serve one another with whatever gift each of you has received" (1 Pet 4:10).

It's also reassuring to know that my own knowledge and experience can help me achieve victory. Each of us has a unique background that will prepare us to do the particular tasks we are given. For instance, a recovering alcoholic may be the perfect counselor for a person with that problem because he's been there, and he understands.

Finally, we've learned that it's common sense to always have a "plan B" to back us up. Notice that David was not overly confident. He actually picked up five stones from the brook, but he only had to use one. The scripture says, "Keep sound wisdom and prudence.... Then you will walk on your way securely, and your foot will not stumble" (Prov 3:21, 23).

Few inventions are based on the first prototype. One attempt seldom fills every need and provides every answer or solution. Wise people always consider several possible ways to serve in case the first method isn't successful.

These are powerful lessons. Applying them in our lives every day makes this scripture real and allows God's word to speak to us.

11.

Of Fiery Furnaces and Adversity

King Nebuchadnezzar of Babylon captured Jerusalem and carried the Jews away. Among these were at least four extraordinary youths. They were given Babylonian names. Daniel became Belteshazzar, and the other three were called Shadrach, Meshach, and Abednego.

When these three Hebrew children refused to worship the idol, they were cast into the fiery furnace. The scripture says,

> Then Nebuchadnezzar was so filled with rage against Shadrach, Meshach, and Abednego that his face was distorted. He ordered the furnace heated up seven times more than was customary and ordered some of the strongest guards in his army to bind Shadrach, Meshach, and Abednego and to throw them into the furnace of blazing fire. So the men were bound, still wearing their tunics, their trousers, their hats, and their other garments, and they were thrown into the furnace of blazing fire. Because the king's command was urgent and the furnace was so overheated, the raging flames killed the men who lifted Shadrach, Meshach, and Abednego. But the three men, Shadrach, Meshach, and Abednego, fell down, bound, into the furnace of blazing fire. Then King Nebuchadnezzar was astonished and rose up quickly. He said to his counselors, "Was it not three men that we threw bound into the fire?" They answered the king, "True, O king." He replied, "But I see four men unbound, walking in the middle of the fire, and they are not hurt, and the fourth has the appearance of a god." Nebuchadnezzar then approached the door of the furnace of blazing fire and said, "Shadrach, Meshach, and

Abednego, servants of the Most High God, come out! Come here!" So Shadrach, Meshach, and Abednego came out from the fire. And the satraps, the prefects, the governors, and the king's counselors gathered together and saw that the fire had not had any power over the bodies of those men; the hair of their heads was not singed, their tunics were not scorched, and not even the smell of fire came from them. Nebuchadnezzar said, "Blessed be the God of Shadrach, Meshach, and Abednego, who has sent his angel and delivered his servants who trusted in him. They disobeyed the king's command and yielded up their bodies rather than serve and worship any god except their own God. (Dan 3:19–28)

Now, what is the purpose of this passage? What deeper meaning is it trying to express? Most importantly, how can it speak to us today?

Well, we may not have been thrown into fiery furnaces, but all of us have encountered heated situations. All of us have been in dangerous places. All of us have experienced painful episodes. Therefore, it's obvious that the purpose of this story is to teach us an important lesson about how to handle adversity.

A doctor said, "Whenever I have an elderly person in my office, I often introduce them to my medical students. I walk in and say, 'I guess you've had a tough life.'

And the answer is usually, 'No, I've had a good life. That's why I'm ninety-five.'

'But,' I say, 'didn't your house burn down?'

'Yes.'

'Didn't your business go bankrupt?'

'Yes.'

'Didn't your youngest son die?'

'Yes.'

'Haven't you lost your spouse?'

'Yes.'

And then they'll say, 'Gee, I guess I have had a tough life.'"

People like this have learned to cope with adversity. These loving, giving and happy individuals have taken advantage of the never-ending sources of support and hope that God has given them. They know that through our pain we can find healing. Survivors react positively and live successful lives. Others react differently.

The same doctor tells of another lady who kept coming into his office complaining about how sick she was and how many troubles she was having. He said, "I told her she should go back to her neighborhood and find someone sicker than she was and with more troubles than she had. Then, if she would help that person, she'd feel better. When she came back to my office two weeks later, I asked her what happened. Her angry reply was, 'I went through the whole community, and there's nobody there sicker than I am and with more problems than I have.'"

People like her need their tribulations. They use their misery. They emphasize the negative and enjoy their adversity. They live unsuccessful lives.

You see, the same furnace that destroys some people matures other people. It isn't the heat of the furnace that determines the results; it's the quality of the people. Ernest Hemingway said, "The world breaks everyone, and afterward some become strong at the broken places."

Even the biological development of animals demonstrates this process. For one kind of danger, a species may develop a shell, another a sting, another a poison, another a protective coloration. To breathe in the sea a creature develops gills. To breathe when it's stranded on land a creature develops lungs. The life principle includes the ability to adapt to circumstances in order to overcome adversity.

The survival instinct reveals a wealth of potentiality that's astounding to those who analyze it. It's the same with us as individuals. We need to experience difficulties. Those people who have gone through disasters have a philosophy of life and a depth of wisdom that ordinary people who have never suffered don't have.

One woman, hospitalized for months following an accident, said, "We only advance through tribulation."

A young wife and mother who died of lupus at age thirty-four wrote, "Even our tribulations can be used by God for his glory and our good. I've gained a deep, soul-reassuring knowledge that whatever my situation, God is with me."

One tourist who visited the Grand Canyon initially observed the scene from the heights of the south rim. At the time he believed this panoramic spectacle had to be the most impressive view of the canyon. Later, however, he hiked seven miles downward until he reached the floor of the canyon and the turbulent waters of the Colorado River. He said, "It was only then that I fully appreciated the majesty of one of the seven natural wonders of the world."

The moral is that you have to reach the depths before you can truly appreciate the heights. Going through a bad experience deepens our faith and strengthens our character. Unfortunately, hearing other people's stories and reading heroic historical accounts are of little value. There are some things we cannot learn by example. We must learn these by experience.

So what is your fiery furnace? How do you handle tribulation? Have you ever been in a real crisis? Have you ever faced a life-threatening situation? If so, what did you learn from your period of adversity? How have you grown because of it? Life eventually questions all of us.

In order to survive and thrive, we need a positive attitude and an unshakable conviction that, regardless of the circumstances, God can help us triumph over our troubles. That affirming faith was typical of Viktor Frankl, a bold and courageous Jewish psychiatrist who was imprisoned in Auschwitz during the Holocaust. He said, "The last great human freedom is the ability to choose one's attitude in any given circumstance." You can spend all your time at a personal pity party that will destroy your contentment, or you can choose to rejoice, whatever the circumstances. Paul would agree. He said, "I am now rejoicing in my sufferings for your sake" (Col 1:24).

Once, a woman moved to West Texas to teach in a university. She came from the beautiful state of Kentucky, where the green trees tower into the sky and the bluegrass grows in lush abundance. She now lives where the dust blows constantly because there are only a few little sage brush and scrubby Mesquites to restrain it. One day, someone asked her, half dreading her response, "How do you like it out here?" She smiled and replied, "Oh, I love it! I just love it! All those tall trees in Kentucky would get in the way of these beautiful West Texas sunsets." This optimistic individual had looked past the dirt, the scrubby trees, and the tumbleweeds and focused on the glorious sunsets. She had simply reframed her situation to bring out its best qualities.

Now, what have we learned from this account of Shadrach, Meshach, and Abednego and the fiery furnace? Unfortunately, the only thing most people know about this exciting story is that a group of men with funny names escaped a fire. If that's all we know, we've totally missed God's word to us.

Remember, Paul said, "Scripture is inspired by God and is useful for teaching" (2 Tim 3:16).

To make this scripture useful in our lives, we must discover and apply the deeper moral teachings. We must get beyond the literal words to the meaning.

First, we've learned that no one can avoid trouble. No one can escape hard times. Every Christian will face decisive moments. Everyone will encounter tough choices that will test their faith. The scripture tells us that Paul and Barnabas "strengthened the souls of the disciples and encouraged them to continue in the faith, saying, 'It is through many persecutions that we must enter the kingdom of God'" (Acts 14:22).

We must accept the fact that life is not fair! Bad things happen to good people. Friends will hurt us. Things will break. Losses will occur, and grief is inevitable! These are the difficult realities we must face.

Next, we've learned that adversity makes us stronger and helps us develop wisdom and empathy. The scripture says, "Before I was humbled I went astray, but now I keep your word" (Ps 119:67). This scripture has both positive and negative elements. It gives us both hope and anxiety. All of us desire to grow and become more understanding and disciplined. But none of us desires to go through the necessary adversity that provides these qualities.

Finally, we've learned that our example of standing firm in our faith will be a witness to others, as it was to Nebuchadnezzar. The display of courage in the face of adversity caused him to say, "There is no other god who is able to deliver in this way" (Dan 3:29).

Jesus said, "You are the light of the world.... Let your light shine before others, so that they may see your good works and give glory to your Father in heaven" (Matt 5:14, 16).

There is a history of dedicated martyrs who suffered for their faith. Stephen's painful death influenced Paul. Jesus's crucifixion has enabled millions of believers to be faithful.

Are you a positive survivor? Can you go into a fiery trial and come out a better person?

These are powerful lessons. Applying them in our lives every day makes the scripture real and allows God's word to speak to us.

12.

Of Lions and Courage

Everybody knows the story about Daniel and the lions' den. Daniel possessed such exceptional qualities that the king planned to set him over the whole kingdom. This made some men jealous. They knew Daniel prayed to God, so they tricked the king into decreeing that he was the only one who should be worshiped.

When Daniel learned of the decree, he went home to his upstairs room where the windows opened toward Jerusalem. Three times a day he got down on his knees and prayed, just as he had done before.

The jealous men told the king about Daniel's defiance. The king was greatly distressed; he wanted to rescue Daniel, but the men reminded him of his decree.

So the king gave the order, and they brought Daniel and threw him into the lions' den. The king said to Daniel, "May your God, whom you serve continually, rescue you!"

The king spent the night without eating or sleeping. The following morning, the king hurried to the lions' den. When he called to Daniel, Daniel answered, "My God shut the mouths of the lions. They have not hurt me."

The king was overjoyed and gave orders to lift Daniel out of the den. No wound was found on him because he had trusted in his God. Then King Darius wrote to all the men throughout the land, "I issue a decree that in every part of my kingdom people must fear and reverence the God of Daniel. For he is the living God" (see Dan 6:3–26).

Now, what is the purpose of this passage? What deeper meaning is it trying to express? Most importantly, how can it speak to us today?

Well, there aren't many lions in our cities, and those in the mountains aren't kept in dens. Therefore, your chance of being thrown into such a place is very unlikely. But if we go deeper into this story, we'll be able to find God's message for us. It's obvious that the purpose of this story is to teach us an important lesson about exhibiting courage in the face of persecution and unfair treatment.

Daniel was honest and capable. That's why King Darius put him in a place of honor. But that made a group of magicians and astrologers jealous, and they plotted his downfall. They urged the king to issue a decree that those who prayed to any other God or man except him would be cast into the lions' den. Since the conspirators were aware of Daniel's prayer habits, they knew he would be punished. They had already prepared such a document and urged him to sign it immediately. Ignorant of the real intent of the decree, the king signed the document.

Their plot was successful, and Daniel was thrown into the lion's den. When the king realized he had been duped, he hurried out to see if Daniel was alive. To his amazement he heard the voice of the prophet saying, "My God has sent his angel and has shut the lions' mouths, that they have not hurt me." Instantly, Darius ordered Daniel's release, and the men who had tricked him were themselves thrown into the den of lions.

So what can we learn from this story? As one of the best-known narratives of the Bible, "Daniel in the lion's den" deals with fear, faith, and courage. It demonstrates the relationship between crises and trust.

Now, fear is a universal emotion. Everyone is afraid of something. The only people who will not admit they are afraid are those who are dishonest.

Furthermore, some fear is legitimate. It can be life-preserving. If people didn't have a reasonable and healthy concern about danger, they wouldn't survive.

Even so, the scriptures say, "Fear not," over and over again, because excessive and useless fears sap our strength and destroy our effectiveness. Anxieties and threats are all around us.

What is your greatest fear?

For some of us, the name of our fear is *illness*. The most frightening words in the world can be looked up in a medical dictionary: Alzheimer's, strokes, cancer.

For some of us, the name of our fear is *failure*. We are afraid we will not measure up. We are afraid someone we care about will reject us.

For some of us, the name of our fear is *financial insecurity*. "How will we pay these bills? How can we handle this mortgage? How are we going to send the children to college? How will we ever be able to retire?

The name of a very common fear may be *violence*. A company in New York city is selling bulletproof coats and bookbags for grade-school children. Deadbolt locks are common in our cities. We cringe at the terrorism headlines and warn our children.

We may fear we will lose our job. We may fear we will die before our time. We may fear we will lose our health and independence. We may fear our lives somehow do not really matter. We may fear God will not receive us.

There is no shortage of fears. There are as many fears as there are people.

So what do we do with our fear? We can begin by realizing that many of the things that we worry about never happen. A wise man said, "Neither our greatest dreams nor our worst fears are likely to come true." Some of us spend entirely too much of our time running from false enemies, hiding from unreal troubles, and dreading imaginary diseases.

On the other hand, some of our worst fears do come true. Sooner or later, most people will find themselves in a real crisis. How do you live when you are scared to death? Well, the best place to start is by telling the truth. Admitting you have a phobia doesn't make your trouble evaporate, but it does shrink it down to its true size. Talking about your panic attacks will help you understand them. Denying doesn't work, and all the protests to the contrary will not eliminate your fears. So tell the truth to yourself. Tell the truth to God. Tell the truth to those you love and trust.

After you tell the truth, be prepared to hear the truth. Listen to good advice. Get factual information about real dangers, and believe in yourselves.

An old story tells of a child who was being bullied. One day, his grandmother gave him a little medal and told him it would make him invincible. The next time the town bully started to push him around, he clobbered him. Soon he was considered the most daring kid in the community.

When his grandmother felt he had overcome his timidity and vulnerability, she told him the truth—the talisman was merely a piece of old junk. All he had really needed was confidence and faith in himself.

Faith in God is also important. He is with us, not at a distance from us. He is for us, not against us. He is supporting us, not forsaking us. We are promised an eternity in the presence of God where there is no more sorrow, no more pain, no more crying, no more death, and no more fear.

Daniel knew dawn would break, morning would come, and deliverance would occur, and that held him through the dark night. So what lions do you need to tame? What worries and anxieties are keeping you from achieving your potential?

Analyze your hidden fears. Admit them and deal with them. Be prepared to act courageously in the face of danger. Don't compromise your beliefs. Don't violate your moral principles.

Daniel didn't let threats destroy his witness. He didn't let fears nullify his commitment to truth. He stood firm in a crisis, and you can too!

Now, what have we learned from this account of Daniel in the lions' den? Unfortunately, the only thing most people know about this popular story is that the lions did not kill Daniel. If that's all we know, we've totally missed God's word to us.

Remember, Paul said, "Scripture is inspired by God and is useful for teaching" (2 Tim 3:16).

To make this scripture useful in our lives, we must discover and apply the deeper moral teachings. We must get beyond the literal words to the meaning.

First, we've learned never to cave in to pressure. Daniel kept praying in his window after the law against prayer was enacted. Paul said, "Keep alert; stand firm in the faith; be courageous; be strong" (1 Cor 16:13).

It's easy to be a Christian in a God-fearing nation with little white churches on every corner. But that hasn't always been true. It's not even true in many areas today. It's much harder to remain faithful when your property, your family, or even your life is threatened.

Paul said, "Take up the whole armor of God, so that you may be able to withstand on the evil day and, having prevailed against everything, to stand firm" (Eph 6:13).

Next, we've learned to trust in God and righteousness, even during tribulation. The scripture says, "We can say with confidence, 'The Lord is my helper; I will not be afraid. What can anyone do to me?'" (Heb 13:6).

Saying we trust God is also much easier than really trusting God in the face of persecution. When we realize anyone can do painful things to us, that makes us hesitate and examine our faith. In some cases anyone can imprison you, torture you, and even kill you.

Finally, we've learned that if we have the courage to remain true, our witness will influence others and change the world. Because of Daniel's courage, Darius became a believer and wrote a letter to all nations advising them to worship the true God. When we suffer hardships with courage, we can also be an example to unbelievers. Peter said, "If you endure when you are beaten for doing wrong, what credit is that? But if you endure when you do good and suffer for it, this is a commendable thing before God. For to this you have been called, because Christ also suffered for you, leaving you an example, so that you should follow in his steps" (1 Pet 2:20–21).

Facing persecution and danger today is more common in some nations than in others. When Christians are a minority, they are more likely to suffer. But even in America, being openly faithful to our beliefs and moral standards requires great discipline and dedication.

These are powerful lessons. Applying them in our lives every day makes this scripture real and allows God's word to speak to us.

13.

Of Handwriting and Warnings

When Nebuchadnezzar died, King Belshazzar gave a feast and openly desecrated the sacred golden vessels taken from the temple in Jerusalem. During the revelry and mockery something unusual happened. Strange words appeared on the wall: Mene, Mene, Tekel, Upharsin. The words were in Aramaic, and the king had no idea what they meant.

When the wise men were unable to interpret them, the queen remembered Daniel's reputation for wisdom. Belshazzar sent for him and commanded, "Now if you are able to read the writing and tell me its interpretation, you shall be clothed in purple, have a chain of gold around your neck, and rank third in the kingdom" (Dan 5:16).

Daniel would not accept payment for delivering God's warning, but he was willing to read the riddle. He told the king that the word *Mene* means "to count." It indicated that God had numbered the days of the kingdom and had brought it to an end.

Tekel means "to weigh." It warned that the king had been weighed on the scales of God's justice and did not measure up.

Pharsin means "to divide." It foretold that the kingdom had been divided between the Medes and the Persians.

Daniel did not hesitate or mince words. He spoke directly to the king: "They mean that you, O king, have been weighed in the balance and have been found wanting. The kingdom shall fall to your enemies: to the Medes and to the Persians." That same night Darius, the median, with his conquering armies, proclaimed himself master of Babylon (see Dan 6:25–30).

Now, what is the purpose of this passage? What deeper meaning is it trying to express?

Most importantly, how can it speak to us today?

Well, we will probably never see foreign words leaving mysterious messages, but when we say, "He saw the handwriting on the wall," we usually mean some clear advice has been given. It's obvious that the purpose of this story is to teach us a lesson and emphasize the significance of warnings.

All of us receive cautions and admonishments. Things happen in our lives that remind us we will be judged and evaluated. Crises occur that cause us to realize that our decisions, words, and actions do matter. Such pivotal, momentous events provide information and direction. The scriptures say, "[God] will be our guide forever" (Ps 48:14).

Isaiah said, "The LORD will guide you continually" (Isa 58:11).

Well, God does warn and guide us, but how do such warnings come, and why are they difficult to understand? It's possible we are so blind, so unaware, and so spiritually insensitive that we literally don't see or hear the words of wisdom. When something is too much with us, we tend to ignore it. For instance, if you tried to write a description of a dollar bill, you'd probably have some trouble. What kind of numerals does it have? What does the insignia look like? What details are visible on the human face?

We see, fold, and touch money almost every day. You would think anyone who has observed and handled something that many times would know what it looks like. Even so, you'd probably make mistakes in describing that bill. You'd probably leave out something or get something wrong.

The reason we don't remember details is because we only consider money when we want to buy something or make a payment. We don't really see it. We look at things all the time without really seeing them.

On the other hand, we may see and hear and even understand a warning but then deliberately choose to ignore and suppress the information.

Dr. Scott Peck says in *People of the Lie*, "The central defect of evil is not the sin but the refusal to acknowledge it." Like Belshazzar, when the handwriting on the wall exposes us or tells us something unpleasant, we don't want to deal with it (Simon and Schuster, 1983, 69-70).

Dr. Peck also says, "Many evil people are not designated as criminals. Too often they are considered to be solid citizens. How can this be? How can they be evil and not be called criminals? The answer has to do with labels. These individuals may be criminals in that they have no reverence for life, they hurt people, they destroy nature, but their attitudes, words, and deeds are so subtle and covert that they cannot clearly be labeled as crimes."

He said, "I have spent a lot of time working in prisons with designated criminals. Almost never have I experienced these men and women to be completely and absolutely evil. Obviously they have problems and weaknesses that cause them to be destructive to society, but there is still an openness to their wickedness." The real tragedy is that many of those who do great evil and cause tremendous damage to society are in positions of power rather than in prison.

Likewise, Belshazzar was not designated as a criminal. He seemed unaware of his sin. When the message appeared, he was puzzled and confused as well as terrified. Later, when an interpretation was finally given, Belshazzar found out he had been weighed, or evaluated and judged, and found wanting. He didn't measure up.

Daniel said, "You…have not humbled your heart, even though you knew all this! You have exalted yourself against the Lord of heaven! The vessels of his temple have been brought in before you, and you and your lords…have been drinking wine from them…. But the God in whose power is your very breath and to whom belong all your ways, you have not honored" (Dan 5:22–23).

Belshazzar was proud and stubborn. His heart was hardened against God's truth. He was an example of a person who had "sinned away his day of grace." John was referring to this when he said, "There is a sin that is deadly; I do not say that you should pray about that" (1 John 5:16).

Jesus said, "People will be forgiven for their sins and whatever blasphemies they utter, but whoever blasphemes against the Holy Spirit can never have forgiveness but is guilty of an eternal sin" (Mark 3:28–29).

Sadly, the warning and guidance came too late for him. We are more fortunate. We still have time. Living with the realization that life is going to end is to live with a healthy sense of urgency and intensity that makes us treat every day of life as a precious gift from God.

The handwriting on the wall tells us everything will finally happen for the last time. There will be a last time when the whole family will be together. There will be a last time when you will go to church. There will be a last time to say and do all those things you've left unsaid and undone.

Have you seen the handwriting on the wall? What warnings have you received? What guidance have you been given? Do you ever feel guilt or sorrow for actions of your past? Do you ever have an urge to change for the better? Do events in your life make you stop and consider your options? Are you sure you have arranged your priorities in a productive way? If you were evaluated today, would you be found wanting?

One morning a traveler in Switzerland discovered a beautiful but secluded estate on the shores of a tranquil lake. Knocking at the garden gate, he was met by an aged caretaker who cordially asked him to enter. The guardian seemed glad to see another person and eagerly showed him around the garden.

"How long have you been here?" the tourist asked.

"A very long time," he replied.

"And how often has your master returned?"

"A couple of times."

"When was he here last?"

"Many years ago. I am almost always alone. It's very seldom that even a stranger stops by."

The visitor was astonished. "Yet you have the garden in such perfect order, and everything is flourishing as if you were expecting your master to come tomorrow."

"Oh, no sir," exclaimed the caretaker, "I prepare things as if he were coming today!"

Jesus said, "Keep awake therefore, for you do not know on what day your Lord is coming" (Matt 24:42).

Don't let your warning come too late.

Now, what have we learned from this account of Belshazzar and a mysterious message on the wall? Unfortunately, the only thing most people know about this story is that some foreign words appeared to a king. If that's all we know, we've totally missed God's word to us.

Remember, Paul said, "Scripture is inspired by God and is useful for teaching" (2 Tim 3:16).

To make this scripture useful in our lives, we must discover and apply the deeper moral teaching. We must get beyond the literal words to the meaning.

First, we've learned that guidance, good advice, and warnings come to all of us. They come at many different times and in many different ways. We must learn to watch. We must learn to listen! The scripture says, "Today, if you hear his voice, do not harden your hearts" (Heb 3:15).

God doesn't always use audible and visible methods to guide us. Instead, we have a conscience that helps us discern right from wrong. We have many versions of the scriptures and various biblical helps. We have the advice of family and friends. We have church teachings available to us. Furthermore, events, occurrences, and opportunities open and close certain doors. Then we have the Holy Spirit within who speaks to us through prayer and meditation.

Next, we've learned that it's up to us whether we heed these wise reminders or choose to overlook, ignore, and deny them. We must take advantage of information while we can. Paul said, "Let us not fall asleep as others do, but let us keep awake and be sober" (1 Thess 5:6).

Even hearing and sensing and knowing what we should do doesn't always cause us to do it. Being aware of the importance of our choices and actions can help us follow through. We've also learned that warnings can come too late for us, as they did for Belshazzar.

Finally, we've learned that our future depends upon our prudence and preparation for tomorrow. The scripture says, "'I overthrew some of you as when God overthrew Sodom and Gomorrah, and you were like a brand snatched from the fire; yet you did not return to me,' says the LORD. 'Therefore…prepare to meet your God" (Amos 4:11–12).

When we heed warnings and choose to follow God's will in a matter, we'll be rewarded with feelings of peace and assurance.

These are powerful lessons. Applying them in our lives every day makes the scripture real and allows God's word to speak to us.

14.

Of Whales and Ministry

Jonah and the whale is a well-known Bible story. The scriptures say, "The word of the LORD came to Jonah…'Go at once to Nineveh, that great city, and cry out against it.'… But Jonah set out to flee…from the presence of the LORD… and found a ship going to Tarshish" (see Jon 1:1–3).

A great storm began to toss the ship. When questioned, Jonah answered, "I am a Hebrew, and I worship the Lord, the God of heaven, who made the sea and the land."

So they asked him, "What should we do to you to make the sea calm down for us?"

"Throw me into the sea," he replied, "and it will become calm. I know it is my fault that this great storm has come upon you."

Then they took Jonah and threw him overboard. But the Lord provided a great fish to swallow Jonah, and Jonah was inside the fish three days and three nights.

From inside the fish Jonah prayed to the Lord his God. He said, "In my distress I called to the Lord, and he answered me. From the depths of the grave I called for help, and you listened to my cry."

Then the word of the Lord came to Jonah a second time: "Go to the great city of Nineveh and proclaim to it the message I give you." Jonah obeyed the word of the Lord and went to Nineveh. After he preached, the "Ninevites believed God" (see Jonah 3:5–10).

Now, what's the purpose of this passage? What deeper meaning is it trying to express? Most importantly, how can it speak to us today?

Well, you are probably not going to be swallowed by a whale or a big fish. But all of us will get calls from God to witness. All of us will have low and miserable times of depression if we refuse to respond to these opportunities.

Therefore, it's obvious that the purpose of this story is to teach us an important lesson about ministry.

When the Lord called Jonah to go preach in Nineveh, Jonah thought he must have misunderstood. He simply could not bring himself to undertake that task, so he boarded a ship and set sail for a distant port. In fact, he disobeyed God and went in the opposite direction. Immediately, a tremendous gale blew up.

As usual the old belief that all disaster is caused by God prevailed. When the ship's crew cast lots, Jonah proved to be the guilty party. He confessed that he was running away from God and told the sailors to cast him overboard. The scriptures say a great fish promptly swallowed the reluctant missionary.

He suffered in depression and misery for three long days and nights. When he finally got out, he went and preached to the people of Nineveh, and they repented.

So what's the lesson in this story? Well, all of us try to duck responsibility at times. We run from difficult tasks. We shun unpleasant situations. But if we refuse to do our duty, we may be keeping the message of life from people who desperately need it. The results of neglect can be tragic.

Once, a child fell in a rushing river. A crowd gathered, a rope was brought, and a strong swimmer volunteered to rescue the victim. Tying one end of the rope to his waist, he threw the other end among the crowd and plunged in. Eagerly they watched him swim against the tide. A cheer went up when he reached the boy.

"Pull in the rope!" he shouted.

The villagers looked from one to another. Who was holding the rope? Unfortunately, no one was holding the rope! In the excitement of watching the rescue, the end of the rope had slipped into the water. Two precious lives were lost because people had failed to do their duty.

Everything we do affects someone else. On the positive side, one complimentary word spoken to a person may be remembered for years. One touch, one expression of concern, one small deed of kindness can change a life. On the negative side, you never know what pain and tragedy you may have caused by your disobedience and neglect of duty. Unwittingly, Jonah put the lives of numerous innocent crewmen and passengers at risk. He also failed to minister to the entire population of a city.

Have you hurt your family and friends by irresponsible behavior? Have you harmed your community, your nation, and your world by apathy and negligence? Remember, there are no private sins. Every thought or word or deed makes a difference. It starts a never-ending process that can only be measured in eternity. Astronaut Jim Irwin looked back at the footprints they had made on the moon and said, "We've left our mark, and it'll be there for a million years." Such is the legacy of influence.

When we refuse to do our duty, we, like Jonah, experience depression and misery. The consequences of disobedience are certain and deadly.

But doing our duty is not always easy. It's not always financially rewarding. It's certainly not always personally pleasurable. Many years ago, King George of England was giving an important speech when someone tripped over the wires of the broadcasting company, tearing them lose and interrupting service. The chief operator quickly grasped the loose wires in his bare hands and held them in contact. For twenty minutes the current passed through him while repairs were being made. His hands were slightly burned, but as a result of his dedication to duty, the words of the king reached millions of listeners.

We need people today who will do their duty. Irresponsibility is rampant. Everybody's business becomes nobody's business. Problems abound, but too many people in positions of authority want to protect their own turf and further their own goals. Few are concerned about others, especially when those "others" are different and hostile, like the people in Nineveh.

So what whale has swallowed you? What are you running from? Are you evading your responsibility? Have you been given a mission in life? Of course you have! Is there something you should be doing? Of course there is! Wherever a particular ability of yours meets a specific need of the world, that's your call to service. God's world is complex. There are many areas of need. Preachers, musicians, and religious workers provide important ministries, but a lot of secular services also provide essential ministries. Science, medicine, technology, business, politics, education, agriculture, and numerous other fields we don't even visualize today will be crucial tomorrow. All contributions are sacred if the Christian is committed. Doing our duty is important.

There is a well-known medieval story of a monk who yearned for many years to see a vision of the Virgin. One day while he was praying, the vision appeared. Just at that moment, however, the monastery bell rang, signaling the hour when the poor came to be fed at the monastery gate. Since it was his responsibility to serve them the food, the poor monk was in a terrible quandary. But dedication to duty won out. He left the vision and did his work.

When he returned, he found to his joy and amazement that the wonderful vision was still there. The Virgin said, "If you had stayed, I would have fled."

The moral was evident! If we choose personal satisfaction over duty, we'll lose both, but if we choose duty over personal satisfaction, we'll gain both.

Jonah's experience with the storm and the whale was a wakeup call. Until you find your niche and your reason for being, you're in trouble. Until you are actively using your unique talents and skills to fulfil your purpose, you are out of sync.

Jonah was in the depths of depression. That's what the writer dramatically described as "spending three days in the whale's belly at the bottom of the sea." People who feel this unfulfilled and miserable often use alcohol, drugs, and promiscuous behavior in an effort to fill the void.

Now, all of us are called. How we answer that call is our personal decision. If we say "No!" we will hurt others and end up in darkness and despair. If we say "Yes!" we will effect enormous change. We will make a positive difference. We will expand truth, increase righteousness, and demonstrate love. Our rewards will be great.

So if you feel you are here for a purpose, if you want your life to count, you must dedicate yourself to kingdom principles by saying, "If the world needs me, I'll respond. I'll do my duty. I'll obey the call."

Now, what have we learned from this account of Jonah and the whale? Unfortunately, the only thing most people know about this popular story is that a whale swallowed a man and then spit him out. If that's all we know, we've totally missed God's word to us.

Remember, Paul said, "Scripture is inspired by God and is useful for teaching" (2 Tim 3:16).

To make this scripture useful in our lives, we must discover and apply the deeper moral teaching. We must get beyond the literal words to the meaning.

First, we've learned that Christians are called to witness and minister to others. The scripture says, "You will be my witnesses in Jerusalem, in all Judea and Samaria, and to the ends of the earth" (Acts 1:8).

We're here for a purpose. In fact, being a witness is not really a choice. If we're a Christian, then we're automatically a witness to the world. But we can choose whether to be a true and loving witness or a false and hostile witness.

Next, we've learned that if we refuse to follow God's call, we'll suffer, and we'll cause others to suffer. The scripture says, "I have made a sentinel…. Whenever you hear a word from my mouth, you shall give them warning from me. If I say to the wicked, 'O wicked ones, you shall surely die,' and you do not speak to warn the wicked to turn from their ways, the wicked shall die in their iniquity, but their blood I will require at your hand" (Ezek 33:7–8).

If we don't choose to be a good witness, we will never be happy or content. Refusing to reach out to others, to teach others, and to be a light to others leaves us unfulfilled and miserable.

Finally, we've learned that if we respond positively and do our duty, God will rescue us from depression and give us victory. Paul says, "I have fought the good fight; I have finished the race; I have kept the faith. From now on there is reserved for me the crown of righteousness" (2 Tim 4:7–8).

We can fulfill our ministry by making a commitment to "let our light shine." This means that our loving attitudes, our forgiving spirit, and our positive deeds will bless the world. Our reward will be a life of joy and the assurance of eternal victory.

These are powerful lessons. Applying them in our lives every day makes this scripture real and allows God's word to speak to us.

15.

Of Angels and Salvation

Everybody knows the Christmas story. Joseph and Mary, of Nazareth, traveled to the city of David, or Bethlehem. While they were in Bethlehem, Mary, who was pregnant, went into labor. She brought forth her firstborn son, wrapped him in swaddling clothes, and laid him in a manger, because there was no room for them in the inn.

The shepherds abiding in the field, keeping watch over their flock by night, were visited by an angel, who said to them, "Fear not: for, behold, I bring you good tidings of great joy, which shall be to all people. For unto you is born this day in the city of David a Savior, which is Christ the Lord.... You shall find the babe…lying in a manger." Suddenly, there appeared with the angel a multitude of the heavenly host praising God and saying, "Glory to God in the highest, and on earth peace, good will toward men" (see Luke 2:4–14).

Later, a group of wise men from the East came to Bethlehem, looking for the child. When they found him, they fell down and worshiped him as they delivered their presents of gold, frankincense, and myrrh (see Matt 2:1–11).

Meanwhile, it had been revealed to Simeon, a just and devout man, that he should not see death before he had seen the Christ. When the parents brought Jesus to the temple, Simeon took him in his arms, and said, "Lord, now let your servant depart in peace, for my eyes have seen your salvation" (see Luke 2:25–30).

Now, what is the purpose of this passage? What deeper meaning is it trying to express? Most importantly, how can it speak to us today?

Well, on Christmas we don't get to hear choirs of angels. There probably aren't any shepherds at our worship services. Rich men aren't likely to give us gold or frankincense or myrrh. Furthermore, very few babies are born in barns or caves. However, this wonderful scripture contains the greatest news ever given to mankind. It's obvious that the purpose of this story is to teach us an important lesson about salvation.

What was this message of "good tidings"? What principles did it include? What gifts did it offer?

Well, most surprisingly, the first group to hear the news of Jesus's birth was a few lowly shepherds. These shepherds were uneducated, blue-collar workers. The leaders in the synagogue looked down on them because they often had to break the Sabbath laws by tending animals. They represented the man on the street, an ordinary group who was not educated and not particularly religious. They were certainly not knowledgeable about theology. Yet the angels honored these day-laborers by assuring them that the Lord had indeed come to earth for them.

The wise men, sometimes called kings or magi, also responded to Jesus, teaching us that the gospel is also for the rich and famous. It's for scientists and researchers. It's for those with advanced degrees. It's for the intellectuals and the upper class, the "movers and shakers" of society. God's guidance to them demonstrates that he cares for this class of people just as much as he cares for the beggars on the street. These wealthy, successful, astute men needed what Jesus came to offer just as much as the unlearned and the homeless.

Finally, a vital truth is expressed by the incident about the aged temple servant named Simeon. He was just one insignificant individual, but he was important to God. His prayers and faith were rewarded when he was allowed to hold the Christ child in his arms.

From this Christmas story we see that the announcement about Jesus's birth reached various groups and individuals—indeed all mankind. But what did it really promise them? Why was the message considered to be such "good tidings of great joy"? What wonderful news did it bring?

The scriptures say that Jesus came into the world to bring a sense of acceptance and love to all people. He said, "I came that they may have life and have it abundantly" (John 10:10).

Jesus emphasized the worth and value of men, women, and children. He said, "It is not the will of your Father in heaven that one of these little ones should be lost" (Matt 18:14).

One of the greatest things Jesus brought us is the assurance of forgiveness. Over and over he said, "Your sins are forgiven you" (Luke 5:20).

Jesus certainly came to take away anxiety. The first words of the angels were, "Do not be afraid" (Luke 2:10).

Jesus also promised guidance and support, saying, "I am with you always, to the end of the age" (Matt 28:20).

It's important to know that Jesus gave each of us a purpose, a reason for living. He said, "The harvest is plentiful, but the laborers are few" (Matt 9:37).

"You will be my witnesses" (Acts 1:8).

Finally, Jesus helps us overcome depression and despair by giving us hope. Paul said, "May the God of hope fill you with all joy and peace in believing, so that you may abound in hope" (Rom 15:13).

The reason Jesus's birth was considered to be "good tidings" is because as the Savior of the world, he brought these priceless gifts to humanity.

So how can we apply this message of good news to our lives? If you feel you are just an ordinary man or woman, working every day for a paycheck, trying to raise your family, then Jesus came for you. If you are a professional person, a business owner, a technician, or even a famous performer or musician, then Jesus came for you.

The case of Simeon reminds us that even if you are just one insignificant individual who feels alienated and lonely, without a support group or a special position in life, you are still important. Jesus came for you!

But how does the birth of a baby born two thousand years ago really affect us today? In short, what advantage does Christianity offer to individuals? What answers and solutions does salvation provide? How does faith actually improve our lives?

Well, feeling accepted and loved is essential to a happy, productive life. When children are neglected and rejected, they become angry and rebellious, and this leads to crime. God's gift of unconditional love is called grace. It is free, with no strings attached. That's our good news!

Being loved gives us self-worth, and people live up to or down to the level of their self-worth. If we don't respect ourselves, no one else will respect us.

Then guilt is a terrible detriment to happiness. Guilty people try to justify their own shameful feelings by criticizing and bullying others. Forgiveness frees us from guilt and shame, and this enables us to forgive those who hurt us.

Living with uncertainty and dread is also destructive. Stress and fear take a terrible toll on us. God can give a sense of peace and security. In a dangerous world this assurance is a priceless gift.

Life is hard. Our technological environment offers so many choices. We often must make decisions without enough information. Hesitation can paralyze us. God's promise to give us wisdom and guidance is reassuring.

Everyone needs to have a purpose. If we never find our niche, we flounder and fail. Without achievement and fulfillment we become greedy and selfish and try to fill the void with drugs and promiscuity. Just to know this is my calling—this is what I was born to do—gives us purpose.

Hopelessness and despair are killer emotions. We desperately need to believe a better day is coming. We yearn for an optimistic outcome. Jesus offers such hope!

As Christians we are loved and valued. We're free of guilt and fear. We have divine guidance and support. We have a definite purpose in life, and we have hope. These are the gifts of Christmas.

Now, what have we learned from this account of Jesus's birth? Unfortunately, the only thing most people know about it is that angels sang and wise men brought gifts. If that's all we know, we've totally missed God's word to us.

Remember, Paul said, "Scripture is inspired by God and is useful for teaching" (2 Tim 3:16).

To make this scripture useful in our lives, we must discover and apply the deeper moral teachings. We must get beyond the literal words to the meaning.

First, we've learned that the gospel message is for ordinary people. The shepherds represented the uneducated, lower-class families, yet angels brought them the news of Jesus's birth.

Next, we've learned that the gospel message is also for wealthy, educated, scientific-minded people. The magi were the leaders of society, astrologers, and even those of royal lineage, yet the star guided them to Jesus.

Finally, we've learned that the gospel is for individuals. Simeon was given a personal blessing. His faith was rewarded. He was allowed to hold the Christ child. This demonstrates that Jesus would have come for just one person.

As Christians it's our responsibility to be an example to all people. We must reach out with respect and love to the "least of these," to the rich and famous, and to every person we meet.

These are powerful lessons. Applying them in our lives every day makes this scripture real and allows God's word to speak to us.

www.ingramcontent.com/pod-product-compliance
Lightning Source LLC
Chambersburg PA
CBHW071010160426
43193CB00012B/1990